T0318069

TRUSTWORTHY

THIRTEEN ARGUMENTS FOR THE RELIABILITY OF THE NEW TESTAMENT

BENJAMIN C. F. SHAW

FOREWORD BY GARY R. HABERMAS

ivp Academic
An imprint of InterVarsity Press
Downers Grove, Illinois

InterVarsity Press
P.O. Box 1400 | Downers Grove, IL 60515-1426
ivpress.com | email@ivpress.com

©2024 by Benjamin Charles Fox Shaw

All rights reserved. No part of this book may be reproduced in any form without written permission from InterVarsity Press.

InterVarsity Press® is the publishing division of InterVarsity Christian Fellowship/USA®. For more information, visit intervarsity.org.

All Scripture quotations, unless otherwise indicated, are taken from the New American Standard Bible®, copyright 1960, 1962, 1963, 1968, 1971, 1972, 1973, 1975, 1977, 1995 by The Lockman Foundation. Used by permission.

The publisher cannot verify the accuracy or functionality of website URLs used in this book beyond the date of publication.

Cover design: David Fassett
Interior design: Jeanna Wiggins

Images: A folio from 𝔓46 containing 2 Corinthians 11:33–12:9 / Wikimedia Commons, © Lakeview_ Images / iStock / Getty Images Plus, Icon of Christ the Bridegroom / Wikimedia Commons, Images from the life of Christ - The Incredulity of St Thomas - Psalter of Eleanor of Aquitaine (ca. 1185) / Wikimedia Commons, Anonymous, Christ in Glory, 15th century, Metropolitan Museum of Art / Wikimedia Commons

ISBN 978-1-5140-0758-7 (print) | ISBN 978-1-5140-0759-4 (digital)

Printed in the United States of America ♾

Library of Congress Cataloging-in-Publication Data
Names: Shaw, Benjamin, 1984- author.
Title: Trustworthy : thirteen arguments for the reliability of the New Testament / Benjamin Shaw ; foreword by Gary R. Habermas.
Description: Downers Grove, IL : IVP Academic, [2024] | Includes bibliographical references and index.
Identifiers: LCCN 2024004993 (print) | LCCN 2024004994 (ebook) | ISBN 9781514007587 (print) | ISBN 9781514007594 (digital)
Subjects: LCSH: Bible. New Testament–Evidences, authority, etc. | BISAC: RELIGION / Biblical Studies / New Testament / General | RELIGION / Biblical Criticism & Interpretation / New Testament
Classification: LCC BS2332 .S53 2024 (print) | LCC BS2332 (ebook) | DDC 225.1–dc23/eng/20240221
LC record available at https://lccn.loc.gov/2024004993
LC ebook record available at https://lccn.loc.gov/2024004994

31 30 29 28 27 26 25 24 | 12 11 10 9 8 7 6 5 4 3 2 1

"In light of the amount of misinformation in today's world about the reliability of the Bible, we cannot have too many books like Benjamin Shaw's to set the record straight. For an absolutely up-to-date and succinct introduction to a representative selection of key issues about New Testament trustworthiness, Shaw's little book is hard to top."

Craig L. Blomberg, distinguished professor emeritus of New Testament at Denver Seminary and author of *The Historical Reliability of the Gospels*

"Sometimes we need basic orientation to a topic. With as much debate about reliability as the New Testament generates, *Trustworthy* shows as a first step that there is good reason to be confident of the New Testament for many different reasons. This book is of special value to those new to faith or for those who have heard general objections to the New Testament and are looking for initial responses. The book also shows where follow-up can be found."

Darrell L. Bock, executive director of cultural engagement and senior research professor of New Testament studies at Dallas Theological Seminary

"For those who are wondering about the credibility of the New Testament, *Trustworthy* proves to be an accessible guide toward building confidence in the biblical text. Step by step, Dr. Shaw lays out an easy-to-understand cumulative case for why and how the Bible can be trusted as a reliable source of information. Readers are invited to simply survey the supportive evidence of each chapter or head into the substantive footnotes leading toward deeper study. Either way, Dr. Shaw invites us all to come and see that the biblical claims of Jesus are worthy of belief."

Jana Harmon, teaching fellow at the C. S. Lewis Institute of Atlanta

"For Christians the New Testament forms their belief system and approach to life. Surveys have shown trust in the Scripture is at an all-time low. When the New Testament cannot be trusted, its message will not be accepted nor its truth applied. As a result, Christianity is facing an unprecedented decline. Dr. Shaw has written the right book to meet this need. His New Testament evidences are apologetic essentials, but his ability to communicate these on an entry level sets his work apart, making it accessible to both students and anyone with questions on why the New Testament can be a trustworthy guide for faith and practice."

J. Randall Price, former distinguished research professor of biblical and Judaic studies at the John Rawlings School of Divinity, Liberty University, and president of World of the Bible Ministries

"Benjamin Shaw's *Trustworthy* presents clearly and concisely the best arguments for the reliability of the New Testament. Although informed by the best of scholarship, Shaw communicates at a level that all readers can follow."

Craig A. Evans, John Bisagno Distinguished Professor of Christian origins at Houston Christian University

"Much of what we know about our final destiny depends on the accuracy of the New Testament documents. Are they trustworthy? This small but powerful book by Dr. Ben Shaw will show you, in an easy-to-understand manner, that the most important documents ever written are indeed trustworthy. That's good news for the ultimate Good News!"

Frank Turek, coauthor of *I Don't Have Enough Faith to Be an Atheist*

"Accessible, clear, and profoundly engaging, Ben Shaw's *Trustworthy: Thirteen Arguments for the Reliability of the New Testament* is a comprehensive guide to the avenues of textual, historical, and literary considerations that can be applied to the integrity of the New Testament. Shaw's breadth of knowledge and clarity of style make this a must-read for anyone with questions about the validity of the Bible as well as believers seeking to examine the foundations of their confidence in Scripture."

Amy Orr-Ewing, honorary lecturer, University of Aberdeen, School of Divinity

To disciples and doubters

CONTENTS

FOREWORD

Gary R. Habermas

Many books, articles, and public presentations over the last few decades have addressed the reliability of the New Testament (NT) writings. Available in all sizes, some of these defenses have defended the entire NT, a collection such as the four Gospels or Paul's epistles, or a single canonical volume. Others, particularly more technical journal articles or word studies, have concentrated on a single passage, verse, or even just a key word.

Careful arguments have been presented across different sides of the spectrum, including detailed evidences that address the challenges to the Christian faith from both scholarly and non-scholarly attacks alike. Some of these writings have been comparatively brief, whereas others have taken hundreds of pages to do the requisite work. Some specialize in the Greek texts, while others treat chiefly a single language such as English. There is no one-size-fits-all solution that meets every need, and strong volumes exist within each of these categories. Thus, many personal libraries contain works that are directed to one or more themes.

When enumerating the advantages of the NT as a trustworthy document, most scholarly presentations typically begin (with good reason) by emphasizing the *textual* dominance of this work versus other religious writings in the ancient world. Such an approach starts with the large number of Greek manuscripts (with the available Latin copies increasing the total numbers significantly) that support the NT as a whole. Adding to this amount is the early composition dates of these writings and hence their close proximity to the originals. In comparison, other ancient writings lag incredibly far behind in both of these crucial categories of manuscripts and dates—even hundreds of years—as critical scholars acknowledge freely. Given that a plethora of early copies makes it much easier for scholars to ascertain the original text as a result, this initial reason plus its subpoints is a very powerful indicator that the NT text can be reassembled reliably. Unfortunately, some presentations do not proceed much beyond this step, with these considerations often being treated as individual arguments.

Yet having this huge amount of information leaves a significant issue unsolved. Even with scholars being able to determine a large percentage of the original NT words, what indications are there that the factual accounts recorded in them are each true? In other words, even if it were possible to arrive at almost all of the original words, it would still need to be ascertained that the accounts themselves were true, especially regarding the most central areas such as the nature of the gospel proclamation. How could it be determined today that these data happened as recorded?

This is one of the chief ways that the uniqueness of Ben Shaw's volume is revealed, as signified by the title *Trustworthy: Thirteen Arguments for the Reliability of the New Testament*. It begins with Shaw's entire approach, which indicates that this work is proceeding well beyond this first argument. The multiplicity of textual considerations above, as powerful as they are, only counts as a single opening salvo for Shaw, without enumerating the subpoints as separate segments. The ensuing "baker's dozen" approach set forth in this succinct book makes it one of a kind in providing such a large number of multiple angles in order to answer the second, more specific question—namely, that there are a variety of indications that the NT record of events is accurate as well. This subject may be considered the chief contribution of Shaw's entire work.

For example, the majority position among recent critical scholars is that the four canonical Gospels are Greco-Roman *bioi*, a *genre* that is a generally factual means of narration rather than simply storytelling or recounting the great feats of past heroes. In the ancient world, this genre provided the background direction for a historical treatment. Next, Shaw compares the *dates of the four Gospel compositions* as indicators that they were composed in the proper part of the world at times that are not only sufficiently close to the events themselves but are far closer to Jesus' life than the accounts of the major founders of the other foremost religions of the world.

Further, it is also acknowledged by critical scholars that the NT Epistles, in particular, contain *oral creedal teachings* that clearly predate them, from the very earliest phase of Christianity. These traditions existed prior to both the epistles in which they were recorded and the Gospels. Most often, critical scholars hold that these usually quite brief statements are dated originally to the 30s AD. Their veracity is confirmed by comparing them to the most reliable sources, both in the NT as well as elsewhere.

Next, Shaw discusses *Gospel authorship* and background considerations that lie behind these four canonical works, comparing pointers to their veracity that are provided by non-NT statements. *Historical criteria* supply yet another angle on the reliability of the Gospels, providing major and minor tests that may contribute to the likelihood that the events in these volumes actually occurred. They include standards that may serve as keys for recognizing historical events, such as having the testimony of eyewitnesses, or multiple textual attestation from several sources.

Undesigned coincidences describe the confirmation that arises largely between Gospel accounts when often commonplace details in one story supply precisely the answers to questions by filling in the particulars in another report, though both were written independently. While *archaeology* generally does not cover large amounts of material, its narrow foci frequently help verify individual aspects that may be quite crucial in an overall investigation or even in establishing a minute point.

More than a dozen *non-Christian sources* provide helpful outside information from unbelievers regarding Jesus and the beginnings of Christianity. *Christian sources* from beyond the canon supply still more data. The dates from both of these categories begin from just prior to the close of the canonical material.

Contrary to much popular opinion and criticism, the *NT canon* of books was not accepted or recognized as inspired because it was chosen by a church council centuries later, and only after much debate. Rather, the very earliest post-NT writings immediately used by far the two largest sections of material in the NT—the Gospels and the epistles of Paul—teaching that they were both authoritative and inspired.

Last, the NT taught, and believers confirmed down through the ages, that personal benefits result from reading, studying, memorizing, and meditating on Scripture. These existential effects are fully capable of stirring the soul time and again at a very deep, personal level. This may include being thoroughly and newly enlightened even when having read the exact same passage a brief time before may not have provided such a personal blessing. Such confirmation reaches beyond the scientific, historical, logical, and other more rational levels by providing a final deep stirring of the soul.

The last of Shaw's evidences for the reliability of Scripture is the *minimal facts argument*. It builds on a solid historical foundation that is supported by very heavy cognate information from independently established scholarly data. Though a subordinate point, virtually all critical scholars acknowledge the facticity of this material. The thrust here is that this lowest-common-denominator approach provides enough historical firepower to establish the central gospel message of the deity, death, and resurrection of Jesus Christ. Even if there are concerns regarding other arguments, this final point sufficiently grounds the core of Christianity.

This brief outline hints at what has been termed here a "baker's dozen" of indications that the NT is a trustworthy guide to what Christians have long concluded is God's book of love written to us. These arguments combine to proceed way beyond the initial textual considerations, showing that these NT writings are reliable. As Ben Shaw asserts, this conclusion encompasses both cerebral as well as heartwarming benefits for the reader.

ACKNOWLEDGMENTS

I would like to thank Dan Hodges, who is in many ways the reason this book came about in the first place. He invited Dr. Gary Habermas, a few others, and me to speak at an event about the evidence for the Christian worldview. For this specific event, I wanted to create a helpful introduction to several arguments related to the reliability of the New Testament that could be done in one presentation. If Dan had not supported this event and invited me to speak, it is not clear that this book would have been written.

There are several other people who deserve to be thanked for their help with this project and, unfortunately, I will not be able to mention them all. I would, however, like to thank my wife and children for their support and sacrifice while I worked on this book. I would like to thank Dr. Habermas for taking the time not only to give me feedback, but also to write the foreword. Several friends, family, and colleagues gave their feedback along the way, for which I am also grateful. Everyone's time is sincerely appreciated.

INTRODUCTION

As one might imagine, South Florida has a very diverse culture, and I was just one of the millions of people born and raised there. What one might *not* imagine, however, is that Florida also has some *ice* hockey players. Well, they do, and I was one of them.

I should note that I was not one of those hockey players who retired and moved to Florida. Rather, I worked at an ice rink and started to play ice hockey while in high school. Though this is considered very late to start playing hockey, I was nevertheless determined to get really good at hockey. Since I worked at the rink, I was able to practice almost every single day. There were several Friday and Saturday nights that I would spend practicing at the rink, many times by myself. The hard work paid off, and I was able to make some high-level teams in Connecticut after high school. I played hockey there for a few years while taking an occasional college class at various community colleges.

After my time up north, I ended up back in Florida and started school full time as a student at Florida Atlantic University (FAU). I did not care much for school, nor was I sure why I was there, but they did have a hockey team. Although the team was decent, the level was different than I was used to, and we played out of a public ice rink. There was no rink on campus, nor we did not have our own locker room.

After my first full year at FAU, I had a friend tell me about a different college that he was going to which he thought was great. I was not terribly interested. He said it was a Christian college and that I might like it. I was still not interested and thought that if I wanted to learn about God, I could do it in Florida (where there were palm trees).

However, a few weeks later he told me they had a hockey team, and this caught my attention. I decided I would at least look at the school's website, and not only did they have a hockey team, but they had a brand-new ice rink, on campus, and it held a couple thousand people. I applied the next day. I ended up making the team with a friend of mine, who was also from Florida, while the rest of the team was about 80 percent Canadian.

While on campus one day, I met the former hockey coach, and his name was Gary Habermas. I did not think much of it at the time. A short time later, during one of my classes, I found out that Habermas did more than just coach the hockey team. He was a well-known scholar. Aside from his debates with famous atheist philosopher Antony Flew, Habermas was known for being one of the leading experts on Jesus' resurrection and developing the minimal facts approach.[1] I began to study Jesus' resurrection more deeply myself, and realized I had a lot to learn.

Growing up, I heard the Sermon on the Mount (Mt 5–7) at a young age, and it made a major impact on my life. However, these beliefs were challenged in various ways as I grew up in South Florida. Though people had different views on life's biggest questions, I rarely encountered people who had any deep or thoughtful discussions on these issues. I would often wonder about how Jesus compared to these other views, and what evidence, if any, was available. I was often reluctant myself to speak on these things, either, since I was not quite sure of my own views.

I also remember seeing Christians being made fun of on TV because of Christian hypocrites who acted immorally. Seeing this was conflicting for me because *it was true* that there were people who claimed to be Christians who acted immorally (and they were wrong for doing so). So those who called them hypocrites were correct on

---

[1]Flew eventually became a theist. See Antony Flew and Roy Abraham Varghese, *There Is a God: How the World's Most Notorious Atheist Changed His Mind* (New York: HarperOne, 2007).

that point, but *it was not true* that this also applied to the Jesus or the gospel. It seemed clear to me that we could only know that they were hypocrites because they acted *against* what Jesus taught (e.g., in the Sermon on the Mount). But beyond that, I was not sure what to think.

I also had questions as someone who tried to read the Bible multiple times but stopped each time. I would start at Genesis and then end up quitting after a few books because I could not understand much of what was going on. If I heard a sermon or teachings about the New Testament (NT), I did not know who the NT authors were, how the NT came together in the first place, whether it was reliable, and how we could know. Though I might superficially understand the point of various NT teachings, I often kept these questions to myself, and in some cases I did not even realize the questions I had.

As I attended classes, I saw that others were parsing these questions and issues at a deeper level, so I did too. I also had conversations with various professors and the long road trips allowed me to read more books on these topics as well as listen to various podcasts, debates, and lectures. Another simple thing I began to do was read three chapters a day of the NT. Ultimately, after I received my undergraduate degree in business, I still wanted to learn more and so obtained a master's degree in religious studies and eventually a PhD in theology. During these years there was lots of studying, discussions, publications, and academic presentations. Along the way, I also became Habermas's research assistant, and now we have worked together for several years.

So what? Why share all this?

I think there are a lot of people out there who are similar. Some may have an initial understanding about Jesus and the NT, but want to learn more out of a desire to grow more in their faithfulness (e.g., discipleship). Some may simply have questions about the NT itself because they have heard others criticize it. Some may have their own personal doubts about the NT and want to know if there is any evidence for the reliability of the NT and, if so, what is it. Still others may approach these issues from more skeptical points of view and are unaware of why someone may find the NT reliable.[2] This book, then, is for people who want to dig deeper into the New Testament and issues regarding its reliability, whether as a disciple or as a doubter.

What I hope to accomplish in this book is to *introduce* thirteen different arguments that each point toward the reliability of the New Testament. I will be presenting these arguments as though it were the reader's first time coming into contact with them. Hopefully, this will help the reader understand the different levels and angles at which the New Testament is trustworthy as well as give a new appreciation of the NT when reading it. Moreover, although there will always be debates—and some debates are better than others—I will try to give general arguments and conclusions in each chapter that are well-attested. More technical debates, nuances, and the like will be provided in the footnotes but these discussions are beyond our immediate scope. Another reason I am introducing these thirteen considerations is that some readers will find some more interesting than others (I know I do!). Accordingly, at the end of each chapter I have included reading recommendations for those who wish to dig deeper on a given topic.

A PRINCETON PROFESSOR ON THE GOSPELS

Many of us have seen the New Testament criticized or mocked. It might therefore come as a big surprise to find that, in 1994, a noted Princeton professor named James Charlesworth highlighted "twenty areas of consensus among experts involved in Jesus Research." One of the areas of consensus is that there is "considerable and reliable bedrock historical material in the Gospels." Charlesworth stressed that the consensus on this point has "far too many international authorities to mention," with each of them "independently, recognizing that in its broad outline the Gospels' account of Jesus is substantially reliable and true."[3] These

[2]Lee Strobel might be an example of someone who was in this category. See Lee Strobel, *The Case for Christ: A Journalist's Personal Investigation of the Evidence for Jesus* (Grand Rapids, MI: Zondervan, 1998).

[3]James H. Charlesworth, "Jesus Research Expands with Chaotic Creativity," in *Images of Jesus Today*, ed. James H. Charlesworth and Walter P. Weaver (Valley Forge, PA: Trinity Press International, 1994), 5-7.

comments may seem quite remarkable to both believers and nonbelievers alike. After all, we often see the New Testament quickly dismissed or ridiculed by various skeptics or media figures.

Yet, if the New Testament is so bad, why would a college professor such as Charlesworth, a professor at one of the leading universities in the world, comment that there are "far too many international authorities to mention" regarding the "considerable and reliable bedrock historical material in the Gospels"? How do they know it is reliable? What are some of the arguments that convinced so many experts worldwide? What about the rest of the New Testament?

To answer these questions, I will introduce several reasons that support this scholarly position on the Gospels while also including other New Testament writings. As might be expected, for such a position to be persuasive globally, it must depend on a highly evidenced and robust case with multiple lines and levels of argumentation. My goal is to systematically introduce some of these arguments and highlight the different angles at which they argue for the general reliability of the New Testament.

RELIABILITY LIKE A MAP

What do I mean by arguing for reliability at different levels or angles with multiple lines of argumentation and evidence? Here an analogy to Google Maps may be helpful. Say, for example, we are using a map and trying to find Miami, FL. We cannot simply look for the first Miami that we find since there are numerous cities named Miami throughout the world. In order to find Miami, FL we must first zoom out to make sure we are in the right country. Next, we would need to zoom in enough to make sure we are in the correct state, then finally zoom in a little more into the right city.

If we were to zoom out and have a macro view only, then we would not have enough specific information regarding the particulars of the city. What kind of buildings does it have? What do they look like? On the other hand, if we were to use only the zoomed-in view, then we would have a number of particular buildings and roads but would not be in a good position to know whether or not we are in the right city (perhaps we accidentally were looking at Miami, OH!). Thus, just like a map, we want the ability to be able to move in and out as needed in order to have a better understanding of the landscape around us.[4]

As I begin examining the arguments for general reliability, I will start from the zoomed-out perspective to highlight what we can establish with some initial confidence. I will then zoom in to specific events and focus on some particulars.[5] Not every argument I examine fits cleanly into this analogy (e.g., archaeology), but this analogy nevertheless provides a good starting point for my approach to the multiple angles we will be using to understand the reliability of the New Testament.

MAPPING THE ARGUMENTS: A BAKER'S DOZEN

In keeping with this analogy, it will be helpful to provide a zoomed-out overview of the various arguments I will be introducing in this book. This will give us an idea of the breadth of the different considerations and which aspect of reliability they address.

1. ***New Testament textual evidence:*** Does our modern New Testament contain the words that were originally written? How can we know? Having confidence in the words is an important starting point to test for reliability because we need to know what the authors actually claimed in order to confirm or deny it. We cannot ask whether a report is true if we do not know what was originally claimed.
2. ***New Testament genres and audience expectations:*** How were ancient readers expected to understand the New Testament writings? If readers expected the accounts to be historical, then this would add to the text's credibility in that it was expected to be taken seriously. On the other hand, if the audience knew that

[4]In scholarly discussions these can be referred to as atomism and holism.

[5]For similar approaches, see Terry L. Miethe and Gary R. Habermas, *Why Believe? God Exists! Rethinking the Case for God and Christianity* (Joplin, MO: College Press, 1999), 248; Michael R. Licona, "Is the Sky Falling in the World of Historical Jesus Research?," *Bulletin for Biblical Research* 26, no. 3 (2016): 358.

they were fanciful novels, then this would indicate that the authors were free to invent fictional material.

3. ***New Testament dating:*** When were these works written? Events that are reported closer the time they took place are generally to be preferred over those that are reported later. If these works were written during the apostles' lifetime, this would be a good sign.
4. ***New Testament authorship:*** Who wrote the different books of the New Testament? It would be better to have sources that were written by those involved in the events or those who knew the ones involved.
5. ***New Testament creedal traditions:*** First, what is a creedal tradition? Second, what do they have to do with the claims of the New Testament? As we will see, these are not the later creedal traditions, such as the Nicene Creed, but highly evidential formulas *within* the New Testament itself.
6. ***Historical criteria:*** What convinces historians that an event occurred? Historians use various criteria that, if met, can often add to the probability of an event's occurrence. These criteria help historians navigate sources they might even consider unreliable, biased, or mistaken.
7. ***Undesigned coincidences:*** Why does the same account look different when reported in two different sources? What are we to think if the two accounts come together like puzzle pieces and form a bigger picture? When two independent reports illuminate each other in ways that appear to be undesigned or unintentional, this can add to the likelihood of an event's occurrence.
8. ***Archaeology:*** Is there any physical evidence that supports the claims in the New Testament? Have any material remains survived that affect our understanding of the New Testament? Have there been archaeological findings that challenge the New Testament? Physical evidence that has survived into the present can shed light on various aspects of the claims in the New Testament, which can be shown to be either consistent or inconsistent.

9. ***Non-Christian sources:*** What do non-Christian sources report? Are there sources that confirm or are consistent with the teachings of the New Testament? Are there sources that challenge the New Testament reports? If non-Christian sources corroborate claims of the New Testament, then this would seem to add reliability to the New Testament texts.
10. ***Noncanonical Christian sources:*** What do noncanonical Christian sources report? In other words, what did the early church report about Jesus and the apostles? Do these sources paint a picture consistent with the New Testament? Or do they introduce new teachings? If these sources corroborate the claims of the New Testament, then this would add another layer to the reliability of these texts.
11. ***New Testament Canon and Credibility:*** How did the New Testament become a collection? What about texts that were excluded from New Testament? Are they better evidenced than the New Testament? If the New Testament was created using methods that depended on and/or desired reliable texts, this would also indicate that the texts are reliable.
12. ***Spiritual and life transformation:*** Is there evidence of lives transformed in a manner consistent with New Testament teachings? In other words, if New Testament reports about Jesus' life and actions are true, along with the teachings of the early church, we would expect to find lives transformed.
13. ***Minimal facts approach:*** Can the events central to the gospel message be confirmed even if the New Testament is unreliable in some areas? Are there historical facts related to Jesus' death and resurrection that scholars from wide-ranging theological backgrounds agree on due to their being highly evidenced? If so, this would indicate that other arguments, such as the dozen above, have greater viability.

Each of these provides a unique perspective and varies in the amount of weight to add to the general reliability of the New Testament. Some chapters will be more weighty than others, but cumulatively they provide a powerful case for reliability. With all of these differing angles in mind, it is no surprise that it is a fact that much "can be known about Jesus with a high degree of confidence, apart from theological or ideological agendas, is perhaps surprisingly robust."[6]

ADDITIONAL CONSIDERATIONS AND AIMS

One of the purposes of this book is to help readers become aware of a wide variety of NT stories, and some of these may seem quite basic. For example, many may be somewhat familiar with the Gospels, and others will also know that there was a famous persecutor of the early church who saw the risen Jesus and dramatically turned his life around as a result, named Paul. However, there will be those who do not know that after Paul converted, he then went on to write several letters in the New Testament. I was one of those people, and when I learned this fact, I found it simply remarkable on many levels.[7] Accordingly, I am trying to introduce factors that may appear elementary to some while also exposing the reader to deeper elements.

Last, I hope to provide some evidential insights and considerations that readers may similarly be unaware of. There is a particular force in systematically presenting each of these aspects since scholars often take one or more for granted in their writings. By identifying each section individually, we can better understand the differing levels, or angles, of the New Testament landscape. Those interested in going beyond the introductory comments in each chapter will find book recommendations at the end of each chapter.[8] This applies, surprisingly or not, to believers, questioners, doubters, and skeptics alike. I aim to present

---

[6]Robert M. Bowman Jr. and J. Ed Komoszewski, "The Historical Jesus and the Biblical Church: Why the Quest Matters," in *Jesus, Skepticism and the Problem of History: Criteria and Context in the Study of Christian Origins*, ed. Darrell L. Bock and J. Ed Komoszewski (Grand Rapids, MI: Zondervan Academic, 2019), 23.

[7]For example, if one were inventing a religion, one would think that only heroes would be used as the primary contributors or that one would only find great feats and successes. However, this is not the case, as Paul readily acknowledges that he did nothing of his own and that salvation was a gift of God (Eph 2:8-9). Additionally, Paul moved from someone who persecuted to someone who was persecuted (2 Cor 11:16-28).

[8]It is also expected that readers will find certain topics/disciplines more interesting than others.

verifiable data in each chapter (with some nuance concerning spiritual and life transformation). Such evidence does not change whether one is a believer, nonbeliever, or anywhere in between. In fact, atheist/agnostic New Testament scholar Bart Ehrman writes that whether or not the New Testament consists of inspired and inerrant Scriptures, "they can be seen and used as significant historical sources."[9]

The value, then, of providing this information in this systematic yet survey-style manner is to help the reader better understand the general reliability of the NT. Whether believers or nonbelievers, one takeaway should be a greater appreciation of the New Testament as well as the evidential considerations that point to its reliability. Indeed, given Jesus' worldwide impact, this book provides a valuable resource as it introduces these topics.

Due to this work's brevity and introductory nature, I will more often than not focus on the Gospels (and Acts) and Paul's writings. I will not neglect other writings, but where space prohibits, I will only focus on these writings. For those who wish to dig deeper, you can consult the recommended-reading sections at the end of each chapter or review the footnotes.

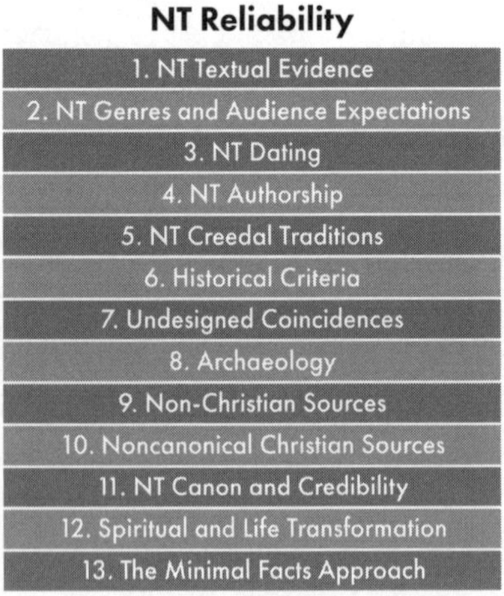
NT Reliability
1. NT Textual Evidence
2. NT Genres and Audience Expectations
3. NT Dating
4. NT Authorship
5. NT Creedal Traditions
6. Historical Criteria
7. Undesigned Coincidences
8. Archaeology
9. Non-Christian Sources
10. Noncanonical Christian Sources
11. NT Canon and Credibility
12. Spiritual and Life Transformation
13. The Minimal Facts Approach

Figure I.1. The cumulative case for the reliability of the New Testament

[9] Bart D. Ehrman, *Did Jesus Exist? The Historical Argument for Jesus of Nazareth* (New York: HarperOne, 2012), 74; see also 259-63.

1

NEW TESTAMENT TEXTUAL EVIDENCE

When it comes to ancient writers such as Homer, Plato, or those of the New Testament, we only have copies of their writings and not the originals. As we might imagine, the original manuscripts (or autographs) have been subjected to destruction, decay, and loss. This can lead us to wonder how we can be confident regarding the words in the New Testament. Are they what the originals said? Do we have the right words?

Of course, having the right words does not automatically mean that the content of those words is accurate. As scholar Jacob Peterson points out, "A *reliable text* is not a guarantee of *reliable content*."[1] Nevertheless, once we are confident that we have a reliable text, then we can test the claims of that text to see whether they are reliable. This is why being confident that we have the right words is directly relevant to New Testament reliability.

TEXTUAL CRITICISM AND ANCIENT WRITINGS

If we do not have the originals, how can we be confident that our copies accurately reflect what the originals said? We all know that everyone makes mistakes, and we would expect copyists to be no

[1]Jacob W. Peterson, "Math Myths: How Many Manuscripts We Have and Why More Isn't Always Better," in *Myths and Mistakes in New Testament Textual Criticism*, ed. Elijah Hixson and Peter J. Gurry (Downers Grove, IL: InterVarsity Press, 2019), 68, emphasis added.

different. Yet how can we know when and where these mistakes occurred without the originals?

An entire discipline known as textual criticism considers questions like these. The end result of these efforts is that when you pick up an English translation of the ancient Greek philosopher Plato, the words you read "do not reproduce the text of any *one manuscript*; editors and textual critics try to establish the *most probable* Greek text by comparison of the different manuscripts."[2] Thus, to recreate the original text as accurately as possible, textual critics will collect and examine the available copies we have. They will then identify and assess the differences between the copies to determine which reading is more likely to represent the original (and why).

Given this process, two components are particularly helpful. First, it is normally preferable to have a multitude of manuscripts to examine. Having several copies allows us to compare the various texts and identify any differences between them. Second, it is generally the case that manuscripts closer in time to the originals are more important. The shorter time gap means fewer generations of copying and thus a lower likelihood of textual differences. From here, textual critics can really get to work comparing the different manuscripts to best determine what the originals likely said. Therefore, two initial evidential considerations that are important for textual critics are the *amount* of copies and the *age* of the texts.[3]

Homer and Plato. With these components in mind, I can now introduce some textual data for Homer and Plato. These are two highly important and influential figures from the ancient world. To give an idea of their impact, biblical scholar N. T. Wright observes, "If Homer functioned as the Old Testament for the Hellenistic world . . . its New Testament was unquestionably Plato."[4] These two thus provide a good sample for comparison.

---

[2]T. H. Irwin, "The Platonic Corpus," in *The Oxford Handbook of Plato*, 2nd ed., ed. Gail Fine (New York: Oxford University Press, 2019), 87, emphasis added.

[3]For proper nuances and limitations of these considerations (and others), see Hixson and Gurry, *Myths and Mistakes*.

[4]N. T. Wright, *The Resurrection of the Son of God*, Christian Origins and the Question of God 3 (Minneapolis: Fortress, 2003), 47-48 (see also 32).

Homer (or the Homeric tradition) dates to around the eighth century BC, with the *Iliad* and *Odyssey* being well-known works throughout history. Though multiple manuscript counts have been given, and counting the manuscripts is an incredibly difficult and tedious task, there appear to be somewhere *around* two thousand copies of these Homeric works.[5] The date of one of the earliest papyrus fragments of the *Iliad* is as early as the fourth century BC, roughly four hundred years after it is thought to have been written.[6]

When it comes to Plato, who lived and wrote around the fourth century BC, his textual tradition has a stark difference. As with Homer, the counting of these manuscripts is difficult and nuanced. Nevertheless, one may be surprised to learn that we currently have fewer than 275 manuscripts of Plato, though recent publications indicate a number closer to 210.[7] This is a startlingly low number of manuscripts for such an influential philosopher.

The date of the earliest substantive manuscript for this famous philosopher is equally startling. According to T. H. Irwin, "The oldest

---

[5]Finding even this general figure is admittedly extremely difficult. See Martin L. West, *Studies in the Text and Transmission of the Iliad* (München: K. G. Saur, 2001), 86-129. West provides a catalogue of papyri for the *Iliad*, which consists of 1,569 entries. Some of those listed in the catalogue are bracketed. West states, "For my own edition I have been able to make use of 1543." West then goes on to provide 142 additional items related to "Homeric glossaries, commentaries, and scholia minora" (130). This list is on 130-36, while a list of witnesses appears on 136-38. Prothro notes several discoveries that have been published since West's 2001 publication. See James B. Prothro, "Myths About Classical Literature: Responsibly Comparing the New Testament to Ancient Works," in Hixson and Gurry, *Myths and Mistakes*, 76n16. Clay Jones offers a count of over 1,750 in "The Bibliographical Test Updated," *Christian Research Journal* 35, no. 3 (2012): 33. Craig Blomberg lists under 2,500 copies of the *Iliad* and *Odyssey* combined but provides no documentation for his estimate. See Blomberg, *The Historical Reliability of the New Testament: Countering the Challenges to Evangelical Christian Beliefs*, B&H Studies in Christian Apologetics (Nashville: B&H Academic, 2016), 644. The Leuven Database of Ancient Books indicated over 2,300 attestations for Homer as of November 2022, but the database ends at AD 800, and not all are manuscripts (some entries are quotes, some are on pottery, etc.).

[6]West does not include this mention with the catalogue of papyri but rather in the w-series (w38), which are various papyri or inscriptions in which the *Iliad* is quoted. (Derveni papyrus; see *Studies in the Text*, 137).

[7]More recent publications suggest a number closer to 210. See Jones, "Bibliographical Test Updated"; Robert S. Brumbaugh, "Plato Manuscripts: Toward a Completed Inventory," *Manuscripta* 34, no. 2 (1990): 114-21. An earlier publication by Nigel Wilson appeared to list 263 manuscripts in "A List of Plato Manuscripts," *Scriptorium* 16, no. 2 (1962): 386-95.

sources for the text of Plato are written in the second and third centuries AD. Unfortunately, these contain only fragments of text. Our main sources for the text are fifty-one Byzantine manuscripts, copied from the ninth century AD onward."[8] In other words, the manuscripts we use to reconstruct Plato's writings are *considerably later* than when he actually wrote. As one classicist puts it, these copies are "closer in time to us than to him."[9]

The above gives us an initial idea of the textual traditions for two major ancient figures. There are significantly more manuscripts of Homer than there are of Plato. The period between the original writing and our earliest fragmentary manuscripts is several centuries for both authors. While textual critics rely on far more than simply counting the number of manuscripts and assessing how close they are to the originals, the *amount* and *age* are nevertheless significant. Moreover, these two, especially Homer, have better textual evidence compared to other ancient writings.[10]

New Testament writings. Regarding the New Testament, two research groups have substantially contributed to our knowledge and preservation of New Testament manuscripts. The Institute for New Testament Textual Research was founded in 1959 and maintains the official database of documented New Testament manuscripts. Its database can be visited online and is referred to as the Kurzgefaßte Liste, or much more simply Liste.[11] The Center for the Study of New Testament Manuscripts is the other important group and utilizes the latest in photographic technology.[12] The Center for the Study of New Testament Manuscripts provides high-resolution photographs of several

[8]Irwin, "Platonic Corpus," 71.

[9]Richard D. McKirahan, *Philosophy Before Socrates: An Introduction with Texts and Commentary*, 2nd ed. (Indianapolis: Hackett, 2010), 1. See also Irwin, "Platonic Corpus," 70.

[10]For those interested in the dating of additional ancient sources, see Jones, "Bibliographical Test Updated"; Prothro, "Myths About Classical Literature."

[11]The abbreviation is INTF because it comes from the German name Institut für Neutestamentliche Textforschung. The website is also in German: https://ntvmr.uni-muenster.de/liste.

[12]Their site allows users to view their photographs: www.csntm.org/. The Institute for New Testament Textual Research site also has images.

important manuscripts, thus preserving them in case of potential destruction, theft, or loss. If one is interested in studying and/or viewing the New Testament manuscripts, the Institute for New Testament Textual Research and the Center for the Study of New Testament Manuscripts will be essential resources.

When it comes to the number of New Testament manuscripts, there are over five thousand copies.[13] This is a remarkable wealth of material for textual critics and far greater than that of Homer and Plato combined. Bart Ehrman, a leading New Testament textual critic and atheist/agnostic, summarizes the New Testament textual situation, writing,

> We have more manuscripts for the New Testament than for any other book from the ancient world—many, many more manuscripts than we have for the writings of Homer, Plato, Cicero, or any other important author . . . along with manuscripts in many other ancient languages (e.g., Latin, Syriac, and Coptic). That is good news indeed—the more manuscripts you have, the more likely it is that you can figure out what the authors originally said.[14]

Undoubtedly, the vast number of Greek manuscripts helps textual critics as they seek to confidently establish the original text. The New Testament is therefore in an excellent evidential position with such vast numbers of manuscripts.

As with Homer and Plato, I am using general figures and estimates regarding the New Testament. This is even more important here because the sheer volume of manuscripts makes giving a definitive figure difficult. New manuscript discoveries, the risk of accidental double counting, loss, incorrect additions to the Liste, and material bias are all factors that require constant updates to these counts.[15] Thus, while

---

[13]While various figures have been given (see below), Jacob Peterson conducted a recent count in "Math Myths." He points out that 5,300 (see pp. 62, 66, 68-69) is possible, but he also suggests 5,100 as another likely possibility (see pp. 68-69).

[14]Bart D. Ehrman, *The New Testament: A Historical Introduction to the Early Christian Writings*, 7th ed. (New York: Oxford University Press, 2019), 23.

[15]Peterson, "Math Myths," 51-58. Peterson notes that the Liste is constantly updating and evaluating its figures to reflect these issues and that one should avoid simply counting

figures can vary and/or change over the years, the conclusion remains that there is a plethora of New Testament manuscripts, over five thousand, and more than any other ancient author in terms of volume.[16] Additionally, this figure reflects only Greek manuscripts and does not include those in other languages (Latin, etc.) or references from the early church.

When were these manuscripts written? The earliest copies are fragments from around AD 100–200.[17] The most famous example is from the John Rylands collection and is a small fragment of the Gospel of John, which is commonly referred to as P52. P52 is considered the earliest manuscript of the New Testament in our possession, with various dates given. Ehrman dates this manuscript to around AD 125, but others think a broader time frame for the dating of P52 is more appropriate and date it within the second century more generally.[18] As I will discuss later, this Gospel is often believed to have been written around the mid-90s. This means that there is a particularly short time from the original to our earliest copy, especially compared to Homer and Plato.

---

all the entries. The INTF also notes the difficulties of counting the total number of manuscripts on their site.

[16]As noted above, Peterson thinks 5,100 and 5,300 are reasonable figures. Peterson's discussion is especially helpful here as he notes that the "typical approximation for how many Greek New Testament manuscripts we have is a bit north of 5,500" ("Math Myths," 52). Peterson provides a sampling of over a half dozen publications over the past twenty years or so. The figures range from around 5,000 to over 5,800 (52n9). Ehrman, too, has provided different general figures over the years. In 2005 he gave a general figure of "over 5,000 copies" in Bart D. Ehrman, *Misquoting Jesus: The Story Behind Who Changed the Bible and Why* (New York: HarperCollins, 2005), 260. This is found in editions of *Misquoting Jesus* that contain a "Plus" section at the end of certain editions. In 2004 he gave a figure of 5,400. See Bart D. Ehrman, *The New Testament: A Historical Introduction to the Early Christian Writings*, 3rd ed. (New York: Oxford University Press, 2004), 480. The most recent number is about 5,700. See Ehrman, *New Testament* (2019), 23.

[17]Some from the Liste are P52, P77, P90, P98, P103, P104, P129, and P137.

[18]Ehrman, *New Testament* (2019), 23. Recent evaluations have sought to provide a wider range (AD 100–200) for P52's date, as adopted here. See Elijah Hixson, "Dating Myths, Part One: How We Determine the Ages of Manuscripts," in Hixson and Gurry, *Myths and Mistakes*, 101-7. For a more technical work see Brent Nongbri, "The Use and Abuse of P52: Papyrological Pitfalls in the Dating of the Fourth Gospel," *Harvard Theological Review* 98, no. 1 (January 2005): 23-48.

There are more complete manuscripts starting around the third century. The Chester Beatty Papyri is an example of a substantive collection of manuscripts from this period. It is one of the earliest that contains a significant portion of the Gospels, Pauline epistles, and more. Ehrman points out that, for the Gospel of John, the "first reasonably complete copy . . . is from around 200 C.E." He notes that while this is just over a century or so from when John wrote, it is "still pretty old—older than most manuscripts for most other authors from the ancient world, by a wide margin."[19]

ASSESSING THE NEW TESTAMENT TEXTUAL EVIDENCE

Now that we have an idea of the *amount* and *age* of the New Testament manuscripts, we can look at how scholars assess them to best determine what the original said. Analyzing the various differences between copies is part of this process, and not all differences are created equal.[20] I will briefly introduce three types of differences that textual critics encounter. Many differences, indeed the overwhelming majority, are easily explained as unintentional errors and/or spelling mistakes. Other differences affect how a text is interpreted but are not well evidenced textually. Last, the smallest group is the one that is more difficult to reconcile.

Category one. As one might assume, and as Ehrman makes explicit, "the single most common mistake in our manuscripts is misspelled words."[21] If we make typographical mistakes copying today with computers, spellcheck, and keyboards, how much more likely were ancient scribes to have made similar mistakes?

Another reason for unintentional differences is the difficult task of copying ancient texts. One example of such challenges is that ancient Greek had no spacing, punctuation, or distinctions between capital and

---

[19]Ehrman, *New Testament* (2019), 23; see also 29.

[20]For a helpful introduction to this see Daniel B. Wallace, "Has the New Testament Text Been Hopelessly Corrupted?," in *In Defense of the Bible: A Comprehensive Apologetic for the Authority of Scripture*, ed. Steven B. Cowan and Terry L. Wilder (Nashville: B&H, 2013), 152-60. See also Peter J. Gurry, "Myths About Variants: Why Most Variants Are Insignificant and Why Some Can't Be Ignored," in Hixson and Gurry, *Myths and Mistakes*, 191-210.

[21]Ehrman, *New Testament* (2004), 481.

lowercase letters.[22] One need not imagine how this added difficulty to copying a text.

> THISISAROUGHEXAMPLEOFHOWDIFFICULTCOPYING
> AMANUSCRIPTCOULDBETOONEWHOCOPIESATEXTW
> ITHOUTSPACESPUNCTUATIONORLOWERCASE-
> LETTERS

Understandably, this could lead to all sorts of inconsequential (accidental) copyist mistakes.[23] As a result, Ehrman points out that the majority of differences are "completely and utterly unimportant and insignificant and don't matter at all."[24] Textual typos are the typical trouble.

Category two. The second category of differences is a little more complex than the first. These differences are meaningful to the text, but the evidence for the difference is not strong (not viable). In other words, if there is a significant difference to the text but it is only found in a single and/or late text, then it is *unlikely to be a viable (or probable) reading.*

Dan Wallace, another leading textual critic, uses the following example. Luke 6:22 says, "Blessed are you when the people hate you, and when they exclude you, and insult you, and scorn your name as evil, on account of the Son of Man." Yet, as Wallace points out, Codex 2882 omits the ending: "on account of the Son of Man." This is a meaningful difference because, according to Codex 2882, the meaning of the Luke 6:22 is that one is blessed anytime one is persecuted, *irrespective* of whether it is for Jesus' sake! However, this omission occurs in only one manuscript, from a later period (ca. AD 900–1100).[25] Thus, while

---

[22]"Lastnightatdinnerisawabundanceonthetable" Ehrman uses this example before noting relevant types of accidental errors (*New Testament* [2019], 26).

[23]While it is true that it is more difficult for us today to read this than it would have been for ancient people, it does not follow that therefore that they were so accustomed to it that it was not an issue for them. With our capitalization and punctation today, people still make mistakes when copying texts even though we are accustomed to these features.

[24]Ehrman, *New Testament* (2019), 23.

[25]Wallace, "Has the New Testament Text," 155. For another example, this time in Lk 1:34, see J. Ed Komoszewski, M. James Sawyer, and Daniel B. Wallace, *Reinventing Jesus* (Grand Rapids, MI: Kregel, 2006), 97-101, 105.

textual critics can discuss how and why this omission occurred, ultimately it is not a viable reading and has readily been identified as such.

Category three. The last and most significant differences are also the rarest. These ones are both meaningful and textually viable. In short, these are the situations in which two meaningfully different readings have competitive or decent textual evidence. Mark 16:9-20 (events after the resurrection) and John 7:53–8:11 (the woman caught in adultery) are the two most well-known examples. Aside from these two, all other textual variants of this kind involve two verses or less.

While we find elements of the Mark and John passages in other texts of the New Testament, no Christian doctrine is ultimately *determined* by either of these two examples (or others in this category).[26] If these texts were not in the originals, as is widely held, nothing about the core of Christianity changes. The central doctrines of Christianity are not affected, and the Gospel still stands. Wallace highlights this point when writing, "No fundamental truth is lost by them [the Mark and John passages]. To be sure, the textual decision will affect how one views these Gospels, but it does not affect any cardinal doctrine."[27]

These two and other textual issues have been known to textual critics for a long time. In fact, if you are looking for a collection of these sorts of potentially meaningful and viable differences, find the closest Bible. Most Bibles will bracket these texts and include a brief footnote clarifying the manuscript data.[28]

Bottom line regarding the textual evidence. What is the bottom line regarding these differences? Arguably, two of the most well-known New Testament textual critics are Bart Ehrman (a skeptic) and Dan Wallace (a Christian). While they have quite different worldviews, their answers are strikingly similar.

---

[26]Craig Blomberg points out various reasons to hold to the account in John being historical even if John did not write it. See Blomberg, *Historical Reliability of the New Testament*, 628.

[27]Wallace, "Has the New Testament Text," 160.

[28]Blomberg provides a helpful commentary on various biblical footnotes, including from his own NIV 1984 Bible as well as those in the more technical Greek edition (*Historical Reliability of the New Testament*, 630-44). See also Gurry, "Myths About Variants," 206.

Ehrman, known for questioning the New Testament's reliability, concludes that "the essential Christian beliefs *are not affected* by textual variants in the manuscript tradition of the New Testament."[29] This is remarkable because although Ehrman need not be charitable here, he nevertheless recognizes that the essentials of Christianity are unaffected. Moreover, Ehrman's overall assessment of the New Testament text is also positive. He writes, "Textual scholars have enjoyed reasonable success at establishing, to the best of their abilities, the original text of the New Testament. Indeed, barring extraordinary discoveries or phenomenal alterations in method, it is virtually inconceivable that the character of our Greek New Testaments will ever change significantly."[30] In short, "Scholars are convinced that we can reconstruct the original words of the New Testament with reasonable (although probably not 100 percent) accuracy."[31]

Regarding various differences between texts, Wallace writes, "No viable variant affects any cardinal truth of the New Testament."[32] He adds that he is not aware of any "confessional statements at seminaries, Christian colleges, or major denominations that were retooled in the slightest because of the excision of any of the meaningful and viable variants." Ultimately, for Wallace, "the text is certain in all essentials, and even in most particulars we can be relatively sure what the autographs said. Further, in the passages in which the text is in doubt, no cardinal doctrine is at stake."[33]

These two writers with vastly different backgrounds come to surprisingly similar conclusions. Indeed, one likely could not tell by reading these quotations who is a Christian and who is not. This is a testament to the strength of the New Testament textual evidence.

---

[29]Ehrman, *Misquoting Jesus*, 252, emphasis added, found in the "Plus" section.

[30]Bart D. Ehrman, "The Text as Window: New Testament Manuscripts and the Social History of Early Christianity," in *The Text of the New Testament in Contemporary Research: Essays on the Status Quaestionis*, ed. Bart D. Ehrman and Michael W. Holmes (Boston: Brill, 2014), 825.

[31]Ehrman, *New Testament* (2004), 481. Though technically nothing in history is 100 percent certain.

[32]Komoszewski, Sawyer, and Wallace, *Reinventing Jesus*, 114.

[33]Wallace, "Has the New Testament Text," 160, 163.

CONCLUSION

Like being overdressed for a party, the New Testament enjoys a textual tradition that stands out in a crowd and provides an "embarrassment of riches" for scholars.[34] There are an incredible number of NT manuscripts for scholars to evaluate. As textual critics have analyzed the thousands of New Testament copies, we can continue to be confident that "no Christian doctrine or practice—major or minor—is *determined* by a textually difficult passage."[35] The result, then, is that when it comes to the New Testament, we can be confident that we have the right words, a necessity for establishing reliability.

KEY TAKEAWAYS: TEXTUAL EVIDENCE

- Textual critics are scholars who look at different manuscript copies of an ancient writing such as Plato or the Gospel of Matthew. Since we do not have the originals (autographs), textual critics compare different copies of these works in order to make sure what we are reading today is likely what the original authors wrote.
- The New Testament is the best textually attested work in the ancient world. There are over five thousand manuscript copies of the New Testament in the Greek language alone, with some of them coming within a century or two of the writings.
- Given the plethora of copies, we would expect differences in the manuscripts of the New Testament (especially since they were all handwritten). The overwhelming majority are accidental mistakes (e.g., spelling). Textual critics, including the skeptical ones, acknowledge that core or essentials of Christianity are *not* affected by any textual difference.

RECOMMENDED READING

Anderson, Amy S., and Wendy Widder. *Textual Criticism of the Bible*. Bellingham, WA: Lexham, 2018.

---

[34]Komoszewski, Sawyer, and Wallace, *Reinventing Jesus*, 75-82.

[35]Gurry, "Myths About Variants," 208, emphasis original.

Hixson, Elijah, and Peter J. Gurry, eds. *Myths and Mistakes in New Testament Textual Criticism*. Downers Grove, IL: InterVarsity Press, 2019.

Meade, John D., and Peter J. Gurry. *Scribes and Scripture: The Amazing Story of How We Got the Bible*. Wheaton, IL: Crossway, 2022.

2

NEW TESTAMENT GENRES AND AUDIENCE EXPECTATIONS

In the last chapter we saw that we have the right words in the New Testament. We may consider having the right words as only analogous to looking at a picture of a map. We can tell we are looking at a map but are unsure what to make of it. Is it a map of a real country? Or is it a map of a place from a fictional story, such as Narnia or Middle-earth? What kind of map is it? The genre of the map informs us as to how to understand it. Similarly, while we can be confident that the claims we have are those made by the original authors, how are we to understand these words? Here again, it is the genre that informs us.

We can begin to understand this element by considering different genres. If, for example, we are watching a *historical* documentary about the events of World War II, then we know that the intention was to present accurate descriptions of the past that involved real people, real places, and real events. By contrast, if we know that we are watching *Star Wars*, then we know we are watching a *fictional* movie filled with fictional people, locations, and events. In short, "one listens to the TV News with different expectations than to a fairy story."[1]

Different genres create different expectations due to the different intentions of the creator. Some are seeking to inform, others to entertain.

---

[1]Richard A. Burridge, *What Are the Gospels? A Comparison with Graeco-Roman Biography*, 2nd ed. (Grand Rapids, MI: Eerdmans, 2004), 247.

Thus, understanding the genre of a work is crucial to proper interpretation. In this chapter I discuss the genre of New Testament writings, focusing primarily on the Gospels. Doing so will help us to know what the original authors intended as well as what their audiences expected.

GOSPELS

What type of writings are the Gospels? While the Gospels were often thought to be biographies, during the 1900s several critics challenged this view. One alternative was that the Gospels were a unique literary work with no precedent. They were sui generis. This view became popular in the mid-twentieth century, and for many, whatever the Gospels were, they were *not* biographies.

In the 1970s the Society for Biblical Literature started a task force on Gospel genre. During the 1970s and 1980s, this topic was thoroughly analyzed, with arguments for and against the Gospels as biographies (as well as other genre considerations). Then, in the early 1990s, Richard Burridge published *What Are the Gospels? A Comparison with Graeco-Roman Biography*, which "called for a paradigm shift in gospel studies away from uniqueness to the biographical hypothesis." Burridge's work quickly became the definitive work demonstrating that the Gospels do in fact belong to the genre of Greco-Roman biographies. His work was so successful that it was rapidly accepted, and "by the end of the decade most New Testament scholars seemed to view the gospels within the literary context of Graeco-Roman Biography."[2]

A particularly interesting aspect of Burridge's project is that it convinced not just other scholars but Burridge himself. He initially set out to critique and challenge those who thought, like Charles Talbert, that the Gospels were biographies.[3] Burridge acknowledges,

> I undertook this study initially because . . . I was unimpressed with the arguments put forward by New Testament scholars, especially in America, to demonstrate the biographical genre of the

---

[2]Burridge, *What Are the Gospels?*, 253.

[3]Charles H. Talbert, *What Is a Gospel? The Genre of the Canonical Gospels* (Philadelphia: Fortress, 1977).

> gospels. Therefore a negative result was expected, exposing the biographical hypothesis as untenable. However, as the work has developed, I have become increasingly convinced that . . . it is indeed the right one and that the gospels are part of the genre of ancient βίος [Bios] literature.[4]

As Burridge looked at the evidence, he was convinced that the Gospels were consistent within the genre of ancient biographies, and moreover he highlights the seeming impossibility of any writing being a *truly unique* genre.[5] After all, if a genre were wholly unique, then nobody would be able to understand the work or know what to make of it because they would not know what the author was intending to communicate. Accordingly, one of the more popular views in the twentieth century regarding the genre of the Gospels was discredited.

The Gospels began to once again to be considered biographies of Jesus. In fact, within a decade or so of Burridge's publication, the belief that the Gospels were within the Greco-Roman biography genre was again the dominant view. Agnostic/atheist Bart Ehrman is convinced and also argues that the Gospels are within the genre of Greco-Roman biographies.[6] Meanwhile, the late James Dunn, a New Testament scholar, points out that the "biographer's concern was to portray the chosen subject's character by narrating his words and deeds. Which is just what we find in the Synoptic (indeed all the canonical) Gospels, though not, it should be noted, in the other Gospels now frequently drawn into the neo-Liberal quest."[7] The takeaway is that Burridge's conclusions are accepted by scholars across the theological spectrum. The Gospels are biographies.

Historical implications. That the Gospels are biographies has significant historical implications. Two of these implications need to be highlighted

---

[4]Burridge, *What Are the Gospels?*, 101. Later, he adds, "It is patently not the case that I began by assuming that the Gospels are biography. . . . I set out initially to criticize the biographical hypothesis" (283).

[5]Burridge, *What Are the Gospels?*, 34, 51.

[6]Bart D. Ehrman, *The New Testament: A Historical Introduction to the Early Christian Writings*, 7th ed. (New York: Oxford University Press, 2019), 104 (Mark), 130 (Matthew), 154 (Luke), 170 (John). Ehrman also notes the difficulty of accepting a sui generis genre (94).

[7]James D. G. Dunn, *Jesus Remembered* (Grand Rapids, MI: Eerdmans, 2003), 1:185.

since the genre tells us something about these works. After all, if Burridge's conclusion was that the Gospels were ancient novels, that would greatly affect our understanding of them. "In contrast to novels," writes New Testament scholar Craig Keener, "the Gospels do not present themselves as texts composted primarily for entertainment, but as true accounts of Jesus' ministry."[8] Thus there was "considerable historical interest" in obtaining, collecting, and presenting the material found in the Gospels.[9]

Since these are biographies, deliberate falsifications or free composition (like that of novelists) were *not* the normal practice for this genre.[10] Of course, I say not the "normal practice" because, like anything, there are exceptions. The ancient rhetorician Lucian shares a notable account where a historian tried to flatter Alexander the Great by including a fictitious battle in the historical report. What was the historian's reward for including this fictional account? He was threatened with being tossed into the Hydaspes River for presuming to fight battles for Alexander (Lucian, *How to Write History* 12)![11]

Furthermore, the date that these biographies were written, as we will see, was relatively close to the events they report. Burridge points out, "Because this is a Life of a historical person written within the lifetime of his contemporaries, there are limits on free composition."[12] In other words, while ancient biographies were generally expected to avoid

[8]Craig S. Keener, *The Historical Jesus of the Gospels* (Grand Rapids, MI: Eerdmans, 2009), 78.

[9]Dunn, *Jesus Remembered* 1:185. See Luke 1:1-4.

[10]Note, for example, that historians could recreate speeches in a way that was considered appropriate and accurate for the situations. Thucydides writes, "With reference to the speeches in this history . . . some I heard myself, others I got from various quarters; it was in all cases difficult to carry them word for word in one's memory, so my habit has been to make the speakers say what was in my opinion demanded of them by the various occasions, of course adhering as closely as possible to the general sense of what they really said" (Thucydides, *The Peloponnesian War*, 1.22. Rev. T. E. Wick, trans. Richard Crawley. Modern Library College Edition [New York: The Modern Library, 1982]).

[11]Other examples here include what Keener refers to as "novelistic biographies or historical novels," which sought to "subvert the biographic genre for fiction." Nevertheless, these do not appear analogous to our discussion, as they "certainly differ significantly from mainstream biographies and histories." Craig S. Keener, *Christobiography: Memory, History, and the Reliability of the Gospels* (Grand Rapids, MI: Eerdmans, 2019), 68.

[12]Burridge, *What Are the Gospels?*, 249-50. It is somewhat challenging to find ancient biographies with reports so close to the events, as pointed out in Keener, *Historical Jesus of the Gospels*, 81.

including deliberately false material, this would have been even more the case when the biography was written close to the time of the subject's life, when people would still have remembered or heard of the events and people involved.

It is worth noting that there are some differences between ancient biographies and modern biographies.[13] While modern biographies often focus on the childhood of their subject, ancient writers did not feel compelled to do so. When it comes to the Gospels, for example, Mark's Gospel begins with Jesus in adulthood, as could other ancient biographies. Another difference is that ancient biographers had more freedom in how they arranged their material. While some were presented chronologically, others were presented more topically. In more modern biographies, we tend to expect a chronological ordering of life events.

Theological implications. Another difference is that it was acceptable for ancient biographies to be theologically and ethically motivated, an aspect not typically present in biographies today. Dunn notes that one of the "common purposes of ancient *bioi* were to provide examples for their readers to emulate, to give information about their subject, to preserve his memory, and to defend and promote his reputation."[14] Thus, ancient biographies allowed the biographer to highlight moral, political, or theological examples for readers to follow.[15] In the case of the Gospels, it is clear that Jesus—the subject of the biography—is the one to follow. Indeed, as Ehrman points out, ancient readers would have recognized the Gospels "as biographies of a religious leader."[16]

However, given that there are no apparent rabbinic biographies of contemporary Jewish leaders, why is there one for Jesus?[17] In rabbinic material, there are plenty of words and deeds of Jewish leaders, but no

---

[13]Keener, *Historical Jesus of the Gospels*, 81-83.

[14]Dunn, *Jesus Remembered* 1:185.

[15]David Edward Aune, *The New Testament in Its Literary Environment*, Library of Early Christianity 8 (Philadelphia: Westminster, 1987), 36. He cites Plutarch as one example.

[16]Ehrman, *New Testament*, 98.

[17]It should be noted that there were biographies of Jewish leaders (e.g., Josephus), but the relevant analogy here is to rabbis. Burridge provides greater detail and analysis on this aspect in *What Are the Gospels?*, 288-94, 300-4, 322-40.

biographies. One reason for this is that words and deeds of various rabbis were typically recorded insofar as they helped others to follow the Torah. Thus, the accounts were intended to focus readers on how to better follow the Torah, rather than following an individual.

Another reason is that the Gospel writers appear to be making a christological claim about Jesus. Unlike the rabbis, who sought to reflect the teaching of the Torah in various scenarios, the Gospels set the life, death, and resurrection of Jesus as the example to be followed. Burridge offers this helpful summary: "To write a biography is to replace the Torah by putting a human person in the centre of the stage. The literary genre makes a major theological shift which becomes an explicit Christological claim—that Jesus of Nazareth is Torah embodied."[18] Ultimately, then, the Gospel authors understood historical and theological claims as able to be intertwined.

I offer three takeaway points. First, the Gospels fit comfortably within the genre of ancient Greco-Roman biographies. Second, as biographies, these works had interest in historical events that other genres (e.g., novels) would not have. Third, the Gospels, within the conventions of ancient biography, are also making a christological claim as they seek to inform and persuade readers to follow Jesus.

REMAINING NEW TESTAMENT WRITINGS

Acts. As our focus has primarily been on the Gospels, I will discuss the remaining New Testament writings much more quickly. The genre of Acts has invoked some debate due to its connection and relationship to the Gospel of Luke. Nevertheless, Acts has a focus on historical events that is readily recognizable. Indeed, as Ehrman notes, Luke was intending to "write a history of early Christianity, not a novel."[19] Keener, who has commented extensively on Acts, similarly identifies it as fitting within ancient historiographical writings.[20] Throughout Acts, readers see the development and unfolding of the early church along with

[18]Burridge, *What Are the Gospels?*, 304.
[19]Ehrman, *New Testament*, 318.
[20]Keener, *Historical Jesus of the Gospels*, 93-94.

some focus on key figures such as Peter and Paul. The focus on Paul may be in part due to Luke's relationship with him, as indicated in the "we" passages (e.g., Acts 16:11-15).

Epistles. Following the book of Acts, there are then twenty-one letters. These epistles are significant for believers and historians alike for numerous reasons, but the one relevant for our purposes here is their genre. The New Testament letters were written from believers to other believers and reflect in-house discussions concerning earliest Christianity.

In *Jesus and the Logic of History*, Paul Barnett points out the value of the genre of the letters:

> The letters are a literary vehicle used by Paul to address issues current at the time of writing in the life of a church or churches physically distant from him. . . . Specifically, the letters are not evangelistic tracts, seeking to win adherents or establish churches. . . . Rather, they address already existing assemblies of confessing believers, among whom the primary work of evangelism had already been done.[21]

These comments offer a reminder of how genre affects the audience's understanding of what is being communicated. The letters originated as a result of various situations *within* the church. They were thus not seeking to persuade their readers to become Christian; rather, a variety of in-house situations caused these letters to be written.

Within these letters Paul indirectly provides important historical information regarding earliest Christianity, the apostles, and Jesus.[22] He does this with an entirely different set of motivations and intentions from the Gospel writers. "More *transparently* than any other writings," writes historian Patrick Gray, "the letters disclose the transcendent hopes as well as the day-to-day realities of the earliest Christians."[23]

---

[21]Paul W. Barnett, *Jesus and the Logic of History*, New Studies in Biblical Theology (Downers Grove, IL: InterVarsity Press, 1997), 42.

[22]For example, see Simon Gathercole, "The Historical and Human Existence of Jesus in Paul's Letters," *Journal for the Study of the Historical Jesus* 16, no. 2-3 (2018): 183-212.

[23]Patrick Gray, *The Routledge Guidebook to the New Testament*, Routledge Guides to the Great Books (New York: Routledge, 2017), 137, emphasis added. Gray also observes,

Thus, while we saw that the Gospels are biographies that present Jesus as the one to follow, these letters were "written to those who are already persuaded to be Christians."[24]

In our world we often see leaks of internal letters and memos. They are valuable because they are considered to be genuine comments made while also revealing what is really believed, argued, and advocated. The New Testament letters were certainly not leaks, but they do provide insight into the internal workings of the early church and especially its historical and theological claims.

Revelation. Revelation begins by with the words "The revelation of Jesus Christ" or, in the Greek, *Apokalypsis Iēsou Christou*. It is a book unlike any other in the New Testament, though not unlike other writings in the ancient world. This work is considered to be within the broad genre of apocalyptic (*apokalypsis*) writing, and these types of works often included a visionary experience (e.g., a revelation) from an angelic or divine mediator, dualistic notions of good versus evil, various types of symbolism, prophecy, and concern for the end times. As a result, a function of this genre was to "encourage piety and faithfulness" in its readers.[25]

Elements of apocalypticism can be found *within* other writings (e.g., Gospels), and within the genre of apocalyptic, there are various subdivisions. Apocalypses were written in both Jewish and Christian contexts. Additionally, within Revelation 1:1-4, there are references to the work as an apocalypse, a prophetic writing, and a letter. This creates a number of challenges for interpreters today. Revelation is one of the most difficult books to interpret because its understanding integrates so many different historical, symbolic, and eschatological elements.

"Most religions do not include letters in their canons of Scripture. And for good reason. Letters ostensibly belong to the category of occasional literature; that is they are prompted by and written for particular occasions" (136).

[24]Barnett, *Jesus and the Logic of History*, 40. Barnett also notes that whereas the Gospels are "self-consciously historical," Paul is not (164).

[25]Andreas J. Köstenberger, L. Scott Kellum, and Charles L. Quarles, *The Cradle, the Cross, and the Crown: An Introduction to the New Testament* (Nashville: B&H Academic, 2009), 832.

CONCLUSION

We can summarize, then, the genre of the various New Testament texts in the following way. There are roughly four main genres collected within the New Testament. The Gospels are widely considered to be within the genre of ancient Greco-Roman biographies. While biographies may be considered a subgenre of historical writings, the book of Acts is part of ancient historiography as well. The next genre is that of letters, which provide a behind-the-scenes look at the early church from an entirely different angle from that of the Gospels or Acts. Last, Revelation is part of apocalyptic literature. This type of literature, not often found today, communicates in a vastly different mode from that of the other New Testament genres. The genre of the Gospels and epistles is a good initial indicator that these writers were writing information that was understood to be reliable.

Table 2.1. New Testament genres

Historical Writings	Letters/Epistles	Apocalyptic
Matthew Mark Luke John Acts	Romans 1 Corinthians 2 Corinthians Galatians Ephesians Philippians Colossians 1 Thessalonians 2 Thessalonians 1 Timothy 2 Timothy Titus Philemon Hebrews James 1 Peter 2 Peter 1 John 2 John 3 John Jude	Revelation

KEY TAKEAWAYS: NEW TESTAMENT GENRES

- Genre tells us what to expect about the writing we are about to read. There are many different types of genres: historical, poetic, fictional, and so on.
- It is widely accepted that the four Gospels are ancient biographies, a subcategory of history. Ancient biographies are different from modern biographies, and authors could arrange the material as they thought appropriate.
- The New Testament is primarily made up of various epistles or letters. These letters give us important insight and understanding into the claims and beliefs of the early church. Importantly, they were written to those who already believed and reflect behind-the-scenes discussions.

RECOMMENDED READING

Burridge, Richard A. *What Are the Gospels? A Comparison with Graeco-Roman Biography*. 2nd ed. Grand Rapids, MI: Eerdmans, 2004.

Gathercole, Simon J. *The Gospel and the Gospels: Christian Proclamation and Early Jesus Books*. Grand Rapids, MI: Eerdmans, 2022.

Keener, Craig S. *Christobiography: Memory, History, and the Reliability of the Gospels*. Grand Rapids, MI: Eerdmans, 2019.

3

NEW TESTAMENT DATING

We saw in the first two chapters that we have the right words and that genres are also helpful indicators for reliability. We must now consider the date of these writings. Were they written shortly after the events themselves or centuries later? In other words, *do we have writings from the right time?* The conclusion of this chapter is summed up by well-known agnostic/atheist Bart Ehrman: "Virtually the only Christian writings *that can be reliably dated to the first century are found in the New Testament itself*, although we know other Christian books were produced at this time."[1] In other words, the New Testament was written within the lifetimes of the eyewitnesses.

In this chapter we will limit our discussion to introducing some generally accepted dates for the Gospels and Paul's writings. I will *not* be arguing for or against any specific dates for these writings, only presenting some common date ranges from scholars from differing theological backgrounds. For those interested in the details of such debates, they can be found in New Testament introductions or commentaries as well as specialized books on the subject. It is also helpful to consider at least two or three different introductions or commentaries as one begins looking into the dynamics involved in dating the various New Testament writings. Our discussion,

---

[1]Bart D. Ehrman, *The New Testament: A Historical Introduction to the Early Christian Writings*, 7th ed. (New York: Oxford University Press, 2019), 6, emphasis added. I will cover some of these other Christian writings in later chapters.

however, will conclude with findings from the most recent scholarly research, which argues for an even earlier dating of the Gospels than is generally presented.

Before getting into the dates, it is beneficial to note three points regarding the importance of the dates. First, having an early date is something that generally only *adds to* the reliability of a text. It is not a guarantee of all aspects of that text. Nevertheless, historians do *not* wish for or desire later sources. Recall our map analogy for a moment. Having a text dated relatively soon after an event is like zooming in more on the map. It helps give more confidence to our understanding of the landscape than later texts would.

Second, I will typically be using round numbers unless otherwise noted. This is because this chapter is a general introduction to dating, and some flexibility or estimation is appropriate. Third, while there is some discussion about *when* Jesus was crucified—AD 30 or 33—I will be using the date of AD 30 as our baseline. Not only does it give us a nice round number to begin with, but it is also the date typically preferred by scholars.[2] By using this date as our fixed starting point, we will better understand the length of time between the writings and the events themselves.

GOSPELS

Before discussing the dates for the Gospels, it is important to note that the Synoptics (Matthew, Mark, and Luke) reflect a relationship with one another. In some instances these three Gospels have very similar wording and/or structure (e.g., Mt 9:1-8; Mk 2:1-12; Lk 5:17-26). This has led scholars to consider how the Gospel writers used their sources (see Luke 1:1-4), and this discussion is referred to as the Synoptic problem.

While Matthew used to be thought of as the first Gospel written, the dominant view today is that the first Gospel author was Mark (a

[2]There are a number of well-qualified scholars who prefer the AD 33 date, and they have some arguments worth considering. However, for our purposes of introducing the dating of NT writings, I will use the more common date of AD 30.

theory known as Markan priority). Some of the reasons for this are Mark's brevity, the similarities of Matthew *and* Luke with Mark, and Mark's more primitive style.[3] Thus, although Matthew is first in the New Testament, Mark is considered by most today to have been the first Gospel written.

Popular dates for the writing of the Gospels generally fall anywhere between the 50s and 90s AD. Craig Blomberg points out that evangelicals generally, though not universally, date Matthew, Mark, and Luke to the late 50s AD and into the 60s, while more theologically liberal scholars often prefer later dates.[4] These later dates are reflected in the following estimations:

Mark: around AD 65 (or thirty-five years after Jesus' death)

Matthew and Luke: around AD 80–85 (or fifty to fifty-five years after Jesus' death)

John: around AD 95 (or sixty-five years after Jesus' death)

Note that although I have listed the "later" dates, this should not be understood as my endorsement of these dates or as an indication that *later* here means "unreliable." Providing specific dates for each of the Gospels with the accompanying arguments for and against is beyond the scope of the present work. Rather, I use the later dates here to show that even with these "later" dates, the Gospels were still written within the realm of reliable texts and within the lifetime of the eyewitnesses (as I will show below).

---

[3]For an introduction to the arguments for Markan priority, see D. A. Carson and Douglas J. Moo, *An Introduction to the New Testament*, 2nd ed. (Grand Rapids, MI: Zondervan, 2005), 95-98. For an overall discussion on the Synoptic problem, see 85-103.

[4]Craig L. Blomberg, *The Historical Reliability of the New Testament: Countering the Challenges to Evangelical Christian Beliefs*, B&H Studies in Christian Apologetics (Nashville: B&H Academic, 2016), 13. An example of two nonevangelicals who take early dates would be James Crossley and Maurice Casey. They date Mark to the 40s AD and Matthew to around the 50s AD. See, e.g., Maurice Casey, *Jesus of Nazareth: An Independent Historian's Account of His Life and Teaching* (London: Continuum, 2010), 97-98; see also 39.

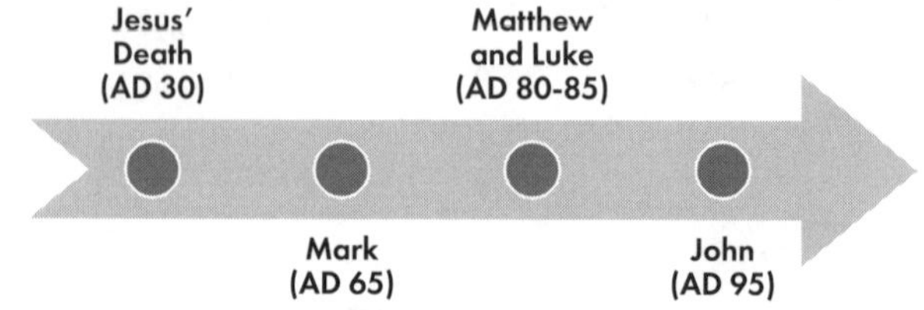

Figure 3.1. Common dates for when the Gospels were written

While earlier dates certainly add historical weight, the difference between the earlier dates and later dates seen in figure 3.1 is not worrisome. First, the differences between the two are minimal. Both sets of dates place the writing of the Gospels during the lifetimes of witnesses (both friend and foe) of the reported events. As Blomberg similarly highlights, "Whether written thirty, forty, or fifty years after Jesus's death, the Gospels were produced well within the lifetimes of some who were eyewitnesses of Jesus' ministry."[5] Second, as we will see below, dates *even earlier* than what evangelicals typically put forward have recently been proposed. Third, those who use a minimal facts approach when possible and appropriate (see chapter thirteen) can use the later dates for the sake of the argument anyway. Last, by ancient standards, the dates of the Gospels—regardless of whether one accepts the early or the late dates—are comparatively quite early.

COMPARING SOME DATES

It may be helpful at this point to compare, evidentially, the time gap between the Gospels and other non-Christian writings. For example, what is the time gap between Buddha's life and when his teachings were recorded? In *The Heart of Buddha's Teachings*, well-known Buddhist scholar Thich Naht Hanh writes,

> For *four hundred years* during and after the Buddha's lifetime, his teachings were transmitted only orally. . . . [By the time they came to be written] it is said that there was only one monk who

[5]Blomberg, *Historical Reliability of the New Testament*, 17.

> had memorized the whole canon and that he was somewhat arrogant. The other monks had to persuade him to recite the discourses so they could write them down. *When we hear this, we feel a little uneasy knowing that an arrogant monk may not have been the best vehicle to transmit the teachings of the Buddha.*[6]

We can reasonably ask, What happened during these centuries? Hanh understands and anticipates such a concern and writes, "Some of the monks who memorized the sutras over the centuries did not understand their deepest meaning, or at the very least, they forgot or changed some words. As a result, some of the Buddha's teachings were distorted even before they were written down."[7] These evidential concerns raise significant issues regarding the reliability of Buddha's teachings, and similar issues affect the writings of other religious worldviews as well.[8]

Such concerns also arise in some, though not all, ancient writings of major political figures. One of the most noted examples is Alexander the Great, who died in 326 BC. The earliest biography we currently have for him is from about two hundred years after his death, by Diodorus. However, the biographies by Arrian and Plutarch are written about another two centuries later and are often considered more reliable.[9]

One important difference between Buddha and Alexander is that Alexander's biographers refer to earlier sources that they used in their research but which have since been lost. Nevertheless, the gap between Alexander and the biographies we have for him is quite substantial.

---

[6]Thich Nhat Hanh, *The Heart of the Buddha's Teaching: Transforming Suffering into Peace, Joy, and Liberation* (NY: Harmony Books, 1999), 13, emphasis added. For an even larger gap see Edward Conze, *Buddhist Scriptures* (Baltimore: Penguin Books, 1959), 11.

[7]Hanh, *Heart of the Buddha's Teaching*, 14.

[8]For evidential comparisons of other worldviews, see Gary R. Habermas and Benjamin C. F. Shaw, "The Historical Uniqueness of Jesus Christ Among the Founders of the World's Major Religions," *Christian Research Journal* 41, no. 4 (2018): 40-45.

[9]Eugene N. Borza, "The Nature of the Evidence," in *The Impact of Alexander the Great*, ed. Eugene N. Borza (Hinsdale, IL: Dryden, 1974), 21-25. Borza names Arrian's as the best biography (22). Though earlier is typically preferred, Arrian and Plutarch provide an example of how a later source could be considered more reliable than an earlier source (Diodorus).

While not all ancient biographies are this extreme, other examples could similarly be provided here.[10]

We can see, then, by comparing the time gaps between Jesus and the Gospels with the religious teachings of Buddha or biographies of Alexander, that the Gospels are significantly earlier. It should be noted that I am not arguing that here are two bad examples, and therefore the Gospels are "good" by comparison only. Rather, there are a number of other ancient sources that give biographical information that is accepted despite having a far greater gap between the events and the writing of them. The Gospels—along with the rest of the New Testament—were written within the lifetimes of those who were witnesses to various events of Jesus and the early church.

PAUL'S WRITINGS

If we find that the Gospel dates are reasonable, then Paul's letters are even better, since they are generally dated earlier than the Gospels. Indeed, as the NT scholar Paul Barnett argues, "The letters of the New Testament, in particular the letters of Paul, are the preferred point of historical entry to enquiry into Jesus and the apostolic age," and one reason for this is that "Paul's letters are the earliest written sources of information about Christianity."[11] In other words, the apostle Paul's writings are very important given the closeness of these writings to the events themselves.

We know from Paul's life that his writings could not have been earlier than his conversion, which is dated in the early 30s AD, and could not be any later than his martyrdom, in the mid-60s AD. After Paul's conversion occurred, he traveled and went on various mission

---

[10] Some examples, both contemporaneous with the author and substantially later, are noted in Blomberg, *Historical Reliability of the New Testament*, 17n33. Contrast this with Ehrman, who confusingly asks readers to compare the Gospel dates with *modern Western* examples (*New Testament*, 83).

[11] Paul W. Barnett, *Jesus and the Logic of History* (Grand Rapids, MI: Eerdmans, 1997), 41-42. Dale Allison helpfully warns against extremes in this vein, which he refers to as "Pauline fundamentalism." See Allison, *The Resurrection of Jesus: Apologetics, Polemics, History* (New York: T&T Clark, 2021), 92-93.

trips, according to Acts. Acts thus helps us identify a number of locations and events while also providing various markers that indicate *when* Paul was in those locations.

For example, we know that Paul was in Corinth for about eighteen months, according to Acts 18:11. In the very next verses (Acts 18:12-17), we learn that Paul was in Corinth while Gallio was the proconsul (or governor). Gallio's position is known to have been a one-year term and scholars happen to have archaeological evidence that indicates Gallio was the proconsul from AD 51–52.[12] This helps us establish that Paul was making his first trip to Corinth sometime around AD 50, and it lasted into the reign of Gallio. Of course, the precise date will vary depending on when Paul's period of eighteen months overlapped with Gallio's period of one year.[13]

Scholars recognize that Paul's letters to the Corinthians obviously cannot predate his trip to Corinth. Helpfully, Paul notes in 1 Corinthians 16:8 that he was in Ephesus when writing to them (see Acts 19). As a result, 1 Corinthians is usually dated around AD 53–57.

Similar methods are applied to Paul's other writings. Scholars utilize Paul's writings and the book of Acts along with other external indicators to help identify the different possible dates for Paul's letters. Though I cannot discuss the dates of all of Paul's letters here, I can nevertheless provide a broad time frame for his writings. The general range for Paul's writings is the late 40s AD through the 60s AD.[14]

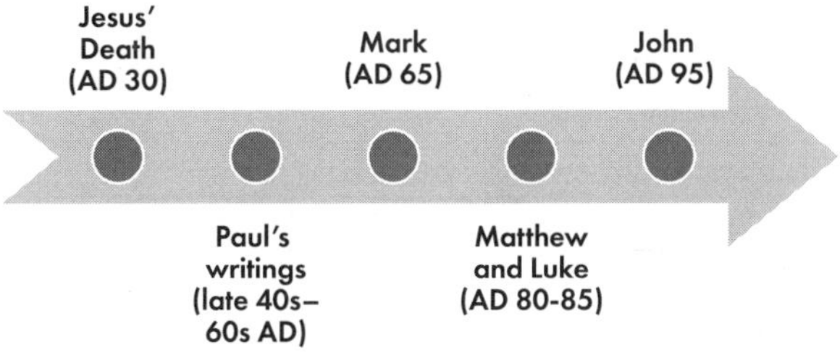

Figure 3.2. Common dates for the Gospels and Paul's letters

[12]I will discuss this evidence in chapter eight.

[13]While dates often vary from 49 to 52, in this work I will use AD 50 as a helpful marker.

[14]Sometimes Galatians or Paul's writings to Thessalonica are dated to the late 40s AD.

Accordingly, Paul's writings are even older than the Gospels, though there could be some overlap if the earlier dates for the writing of the Gospels are used. In either case, Paul's writings provide some of the earliest literary data for Jesus and early Christianity from someone who was heavily involved with the movement, as a persecutor then as a preacher; someone who knew the eyewitnesses (see chapter five); and someone who was eventually martyred. Such evidence has key markers of reliability.

EVEN EARLIER GOSPEL DATES?

Jonathan Bernier recently argues against both sets of dates for the Gospels mentioned above in his work *Rethinking the Dates of the New Testament*.[15] He argues it's possible that all four Gospels were written even earlier than Paul's letters. Though I cannot get into the details of his arguments here, the dates he suggests for the Gospels and Paul's letters can be found in table 3.1.

Table 3.1. Bernier's suggestions for dates of the New Testament writings

New Testament Writing	Date
Matthew	45–59
Mark	42–45
Luke	59
John	60–70
Acts	62
Romans	winter of 56/57
1 Corinthians	early 56
2 Corinthians	later 56
Galatians	47–52
Ephesians	57–59
Philippians	57–59
Colossians	57–59
1 Thessalonians	50–52
2 Thessalonians	50–52

[15]Jonathan Bernier, *Rethinking the Dates of the New Testament: The Evidence for Early Composition* (Grand Rapids, MI: Baker Academic, 2022).

New Testament Writing	Date
1 Timothy (Pauline)	63 or 64
2 Timothy (Pauline)	64–68
Titus (Pauline)	63–64
Philemon	57–59

Source: Dates are pulled from a chart (modified here) in Jonathan Bernier, *Rethinking the Dates of the New Testament: The Evidence for Early Composition* (Grand Rapids, MI: Baker Academic, 2022), 277-78. I am using the Pauline authorship dates for the writings listed, though Bernier also includes a list of dates for works that some have argued are pseudo-Pauline.

Bernier's work follows and advances an earlier work from 1976 by John A. T. Robinson.[16] Robinson's arguments were likely even more challenging to the scholars of his day because that time period had a greater skeptical atmosphere than today.[17] Nevertheless, according to Bernier, the significance of these two works is that they are the only two monograph-length studies

> published since the turn of the twentieth century by professional biblical scholars who defend lower chronologies for the composition dates of the New Testament corpus, while there have been zero similar studies defending middle or higher chronologies. This puts lower chronologies in an intellectually privileged position. The best way to offset this privilege is for professional New Testament scholars to produce comparable defenses of middle or higher chronologies.[18]

While Bernier's book remains to be more thoroughly analyzed by scholars, it highlights that there are significant and serious arguments being presented for dates that are earlier than often thought. If the dates are as early as Bernier and Robinson suggest, then the reliability of these writings would increase slightly more. If not, the Gospels were still written within the lifetimes of the eyewitnesses. Either way, the Gospels were written within a reliable time frame.

[16]John A. T. Robinson, *Redating the New Testament* (London: SCM Press, 1976).

[17]As indicated by the comments in E. Earle Ellis, "Dating the New Testament," *New Testament Studies* 26, no. 4 (July 1980): 487, 501-2.

[18]Bernier, *Rethinking the Dates*, 280.

CONCLUSION

This chapter ends similar to how it started, by highlighting that the New Testament, among other Christian writings, were written prior to the close of the first century. We have seen specifically that the Gospels and Paul's letters were written within the lifetimes of various witnesses. This holds whether one uses the early or later dates for the Gospels. Moreover, if Bernier is correct, then the Gospels were written considerably earlier than is often thought. As I close this chapter, it is important to note that having reasonable dating for these materials does not automatically guarantee accuracy, though it certainly adds credibility. After all, we do not hear historians saying that they wished they had later sources for an event, let alone desire sources as late as those for Buddha or Alexander.

KEY TAKEAWAYS: NEW TESTAMENT DATING

- All of the Gospels were written well within the lifetimes of those who were eyewitnesses to Jesus' life and ministry. It is widely accepted that the Gospels were written within decades of Jesus' life.
- Paul's letters were written even earlier than the Gospels. He was writing around twenty years after Jesus' death.

RECOMMENDED READING

Bernier, Jonathan. *Rethinking the Dates of the New Testament: The Evidence for Early Composition*. Grand Rapids, MI: Baker Academic, 2022.

Carson, D. A., and Douglas J. Moo. *An Introduction to the New Testament*. 2nd ed. Grand Rapids, MI: Zondervan, 2005.

Elwell, Walter A., and Robert W. Yarbrough. *Encountering the New Testament: A Historical and Theological Survey*. 3rd ed. Grand Rapids, MI: Baker Academic, 2013.

4

NEW TESTAMENT AUTHORSHIP

We previously examined the textual evidence, genre, and dating. Our next consideration has to do with the authors of these different writings. Who wrote the various New Testament writings? Are they people we would want to be writing these works? Were they related or connected to the events? Were they people in a good position to know the truth (or falsity) of what was being reported? As with the last chapter, we will examine the reliability question from a zoomed-out perspective. Authorship alone will not give us all the details, but we will have a better view of the city.

Since there is often debate surrounding the authorship of these twenty-seven writings, this chapter will be able to only *briefly introduce* some issues related to authorship. One way I will be doing this is by limiting the discussion to the writings of Paul and the Gospels. We will begin by looking at Paul's writings and see that several of Paul's writings are considered to have been undisputedly written by Paul, even by skeptics. We will then move to the Gospels and consider whether they were anonymous, as some contend, or whether Matthew, Mark, Luke, and John were the original names for these Gospels.

PAUL'S LETTERS

It is an *incredible fact* that within the New Testament we have the writings of someone who persecuted the church. His name is Paul, and he aggressively and violently persecuted early Christians. He was present at and approved of Stephen's martyrdom, as reported in Acts 8:1. He was sent to Damascus to continue his persecution of believers there, according to Acts 9:1-2.[1] Paul also provides us with his own firsthand statements of how he personally persecuted believers in several of his letters (1 Cor 15:9; Gal 1:13; Phil 3:6; 1 Tim 1:13-14).

However, after having an experience of the risen Jesus, he had a rather dramatic conversion and began preaching the gospel message he once tried to destroy (Acts 9:3-31; Phil 3:3-7; 1 Tim 1:12-16). He met with many who personally walked, talked, and lived with Jesus (see esp. Gal 1:18; Acts 15:1-35.) and was a participant in many events of the early church as one who was willing to suffer as a follower of Jesus (2 Cor 11:16-30) and eventually died for his faith.

Prior to his martyrdom, Paul wrote several letters contained within the New Testament. As noted in chapter three, Paul's writings are typically dated earlier than the Gospels. The result is, in the words of Paul Barnett, a series of writings that are "remarkable for their closeness in time to the historical Jesus. And they are written by one who had been part of Christian history almost from the outset, first as persecutor, then as apostle."[2] Paul is quite a remarkable source indeed!

There are thirteen letters in the New Testament that open with Paul's name explicitly stated for the reader:

- Romans
- 1 Corinthians
- 2 Corinthians
- Galatians
- Ephesians
- Philippians
- Colossians
- 1 Thessalonians

[1]See Gal 1:17, where Paul mentions a return to Damascus.

[2]Paul Barnett, *Jesus and the Logic of History* (Grand Rapids, MI: Eerdmans, 1997), 55.

- 2 Thessalonians
- 1 Timothy
- 2 Timothy
- Titus
- Philemon

We know that Paul occasionally used a secretary to help him write these letters. For example, Tertius in Romans 16:22 states that he was the one who wrote the letter.[3] Though Paul used people to help him write, he is still considered the author of the letter.[4] In other letters, Paul indicates that others were with him while it was being composed. Sosthenes, for example, is mentioned with Paul in 1 Corinthians 1:1, while Timothy is present in 2 Corinthians 1:1. These provide incidental details that help us to better understand these writings and the developments of the early church, and these details come from a prominent member of the church.

While Paul does warn about the possibility of a letter being written in his name (2 Thess 2:2), one common reason more critical scholars today question Paul's authorship is style and/or consistency concerns.[5] We can agree with scholars that such objections seem rather subjective.[6] Nevertheless, when it comes to Paul's writings, even the most skeptical scholars recognize that at least seven are *undisputedly* Pauline.[7] As we will see in chapter five, two of these undisputed works, 1 Corinthians and Galatians, are incredibly important for understanding some of the best and earliest historical evidence for Christianity.

---

[3]Paul also makes explicit when he is personally writing: 1 Cor 16:21; Gal 6:11; Philem 19.

[4]My comments here reflect the historical nature of Paul's authorship. Divine inspiration and the authorship of the Holy Spirit (see 1 Tim 3:16) are beyond the scope of the present comments.

[5]Luke Timothy Johnson, *The Writings of the New Testament: An Interpretation*, 3rd ed. (Minneapolis: Fortress, 2010), 241-42. Similarly, though noting apparent subcategories, D. A. Carson and Douglas J. Moo, *An Introduction to the New Testament*, 2nd ed. (Grand Rapids, MI: Zondervan, 2005), 482-86.

[6]Luke Timothy Johnson writes, "The discussion of authenticity has thus been distorted by doubtful premises" (*Writings of the New Testament*, 242). See also Carson and Moo, *Introduction to the New Testament*, chap. 8. The use of secretaries is another factor in these discussions.

[7]A point also noted in Johnson, *Writings of the New Testament*, 241.

UNDISPUTEDLY PAULINE
Romans
1 Corinthians
2 Corinthians
Galatians
Philippians
1 Thessalonians
Philemon

Some of these letters were written to churches that Paul had founded (e.g., 1–2 Corinthians), and others were written to churches in cities Paul had not yet visited (e.g., Romans). As in-house letters written to those who already believed, these writings present the inner workings and beliefs of the early church. Not only that, but they were also undoubtedly written by one who had converted from a persecutor to a preacher.

THE GOSPEL AUTHORS

The authorship of the Gospels is a complex issue, so where is a good place to begin? It is helpful to start with three initial observations:

1. The names of any of the Gospel authors are not found in the body of the texts, as is the case with, for example, Paul's letters (e.g., his greetings).
2. In the ancient world, Matthew, Mark, Luke, and John were the *only* names attributed to the four canonical Gospels. These names were not contested, nor were any other names suggested in their place.
3. Two Gospels are connected to eyewitnesses: Matthew and John. The other two are believed to have been written by someone associated with an apostle: Mark (Peter's interpreter) and Luke (Paul's traveling companion).

Each of these points helps give us a handle to begin to grasp the complexities that encompass Gospel authorship debates.

My goal in the rest of this chapter is to introduce arguments demonstrating that the Gospels were not functionally anonymous. While they are technically anonymous in that the author's name does not appear in the body of the text, they were not functionally anonymous—in other words, the authors were *intended* to be known. I will also highlight the consistency and uniformity of the four names connected to the Gospels.

Anonymous Gospels? Though Matthew, Mark, Luke, and John are uniformly associated with the four Gospels, many contend that the Gospels were originally anonymous. One of the main reasons for this contention is that there is no named author in the body of the work. Paul's letters begin with his name in the text as part of his introduction, but the Gospels do no such thing. Thus, *in this sense*, the four Gospels are *technically* anonymous. However, does this mean that the Gospels are or were intended to be *functionally* anonymous works, with the original authors unknown?

Several scholars challenge the claim that the Gospels were functionally anonymous and/or circulated anonymously.[8] There are a number of reasons for this. First, there are other technically anonymous works in the ancient world, yet we still know who wrote them. Two New Testament scholars, Richard Bauckham and Simon Gathercole, highlight examples such as Lucian's *Life of Demonax* and Josephus's *Vita*, which are similarly anonymous in that their names are not in the body of the text.[9] Yet neither of these sources is considered actually (i.e., functionally) anonymous. We also know these were the authors despite the fact their names are *not* in the body of the text.[10]

---

[8]Martin Hengel, *Studies in the Gospel of Mark*, trans. John Bowden (London: SCM Press, 1985), 64-84. More recently, see Richard Bauckham, *Jesus and the Eyewitnesses: The Gospels as Eyewitness Testimony* (Grand Rapids, MI: Eerdmans, 2006), 300-305; Simon Gathercole, "The Alleged Anonymity of the Canonical Gospels," *Journal of Theological Studies* 69, no. 2 (2018): 447-76.

[9]Bauckham, *Jesus and the Eyewitnesses*, 300; Gathercole, "Alleged Anonymity," 458. Gathercole gives several other examples (455-59). One might add Plutarch's well-known biographies to these lists.

[10]One might add to this that modern-day examples abound as well. Many papers, books, and articles do not include the author's name *in the body of the work*, but we nevertheless know who wrote them.

Second, there is what we might call the *problem of practicality*. Bauckham summarizes this as "the need for titles that distinguished one Gospel from another . . . as soon as any Christian community had copies of more than one in its library and was reading more than one in its worship meetings."[11] If there were multiple Gospels circulating in the early church, they would have needed to be distinguished from one another as a matter of practicality.

This would not have been a problem faced by the early church alone, for as just noted, other writings in the ancient world were also technically anonymous. In both cases, the name of the author could "be noted, with a brief title, on the outside of the scroll or on a label affixed to the scroll."[12] Thus, the Gospels, like other ancient works, would have needed ways to be identified by potential readers while they were being stored.

The uniformity of the Gospel names. The third and final consideration concerns the *absence of positive evidence* that ancient writers thought the Gospels were anonymous. Specifically, if the Gospels were initially intended to be anonymous or the original authors were unknown, we would expect to find a variety of different names attached to them as they circulated (an issue with the book of Hebrews).[13] We might expect, for example, that if the Gospels were copied without names attached to them, then "a variation of titles would have inevitably arisen," as the circulation of "anonymous works without a title would of necessity have led to a multiplicity of titles."[14]

Accordingly, for the Gospels-as-functionally-anonymous argument to work, it seems we would be required to believe the following. We would need to believe the Gospels were copied multiple times, by different

---

[11]Bauckham, *Jesus and the Eyewitnesses*, 303.

[12]Bauckham, *Jesus and the Eyewitnesses*, 300. Gathercole provides seven possibilities in "Alleged Anonymity," 459-60. For other practical considerations, see 461-63.

[13]Gathercole raises these two points of silence regarding the Gospels and contrasts them with the book of Hebrews ("Alleged Anonymity," 473-75). This consideration alone does not necessarily mean that Hebrews was intended to be anonymous, as the original author could have been lost, mistaken, etc. (Heb 13:13, 23). See Andreas J. Köstenberger, L. Scott Kellum, and Charles L. Quarles, *The Cradle, the Cross, and the Crown: An Introduction to the New Testament* (Nashville: B&H Academic, 2009), 671.

[14]Hengel, *Studies in the Gospel of Mark*, 82.

people and different churches, across a wide geographic range, and over a period of time. Throughout this process, different churches in different areas of the Mediterranean decided to start ascribing names to these writings. It just so happens to be the case that they all agreed to the same name. Of course, this did not happen just one time but four.[15] This scenario seems highly unlikely and rather ad hoc. The Gospels are likely to have had the same names precisely because they were not anonymous.

Moreover, as we saw, other technically anonymous works existed in the ancient world, and there were practical methods to identify such works. While there are other considerations regarding the names associated with the Gospels, we can ultimately agree with Gathercole when he writes, "It is a category mistake to say that a work is anonymous because it does not contain within it the name of the author."[16]

Earliest Gospel references. I noted that there is no positive evidence suggesting the Gospels were known by a multiplicity of names. Well, what do we know about the Gospel names? Gathercole provides an excellent and instructive article discussing the names associated with the four Gospels. He highlights about sixteen early sources that refer to one or more Gospel authors.[17] One of the references is a well-known comment from Irenaeus of Lyons. Irenaeus was writing around AD 180 and states,

> Matthew also issued a written Gospel among the Hebrews in their dialect, while Peter and Paul were preaching at Rome, and laying the foundations of the Church. After their departure, Mark, the disciple and interpreter of Peter did also hand down to us in writing what had been preached by Peter. Luke also, the companion of Paul, recorded in a book the Gospel preached by him. Afterwards, John, the disciple of the Lord, who also had leaned upon his breast, did himself publish a Gospel during his residence at Ephesus in Asia. (*Against Heresies* 3.1.1)

---

[15]A similar point is raised by Brant Pitre, *The Case for Jesus: The Biblical and Historical Evidence for Christ* (New York: Image, 2016), 19.

[16]Gathercole, "Alleged Anonymity," 460. Additional arguments include the "inconceivable" nature of a work like Luke–Acts having a dedicatee be anonymous (Bauckham, *Jesus and the Eyewitnesses*, 301).

[17]Gathercole, "Alleged Anonymity," 463-73.

All four Gospels and their authors are mentioned here, with a brief background by Irenaeus. There is no indication that they went by other names or that these names were debated. Other citations by Gathercole similarly refer to the four Gospel names, each with differing levels of detail.[18]

Gathercole's list is also beneficial because it references manuscript titles (e.g., P66) as well as other ancient references (Ptolemy, Apollinaris, Theophilus, Clement of Alexandria, etc.). Significantly, all these sources date from roughly AD 100–200, or around a century after the last Gospel. "Taken all in all," Gathercole concludes, "the first two centuries CE are populated by a good deal more references to Gospel authors than is commonly appreciated."[19] Indeed, his list is helpful because it provides the earliest references to the names of the Gospels, which were always Matthew, Mark, Luke, or John.

Ultimately, rather than seeing a diversity of names given to these Gospels, there is uniformity among the earliest references to their authors. As Bauckham argues, "No evidence exists that these Gospels were ever known by other names. The universal form of the titles and the universal use of them as soon as we have any evidence suggest that they originated at an early stage."[20] Indeed, this is precisely what we find with the Gospels.

CONCLUSION

We have covered a lot of territory thus far, and the conclusions of Brant Pitre offer a helpful summary. The Gospels are "ancient biographies written by the students of Jesus and their followers, written well within the lifetimes of the apostles and eyewitnesses to Jesus. As such, they

[18]In the early 100s, Papias also made a reference to at least two Gospels (Matthew and Mark), and his words are preserved in Eusebius, *Ecclesiastical History* 3.39. Gathercole notes that John is likely mentioned in other fragments of Papias and Luke may possibly be mentioned as well ("Alleged Anonymity," 470-71).

[19]Gathercole, "Alleged Anonymity," 472. Additionally, "The most common attestation is to John and Matthew . . . with Mark and Luke in the lower tier, facts which roughly dovetail with the evidence from papyri as well as with the relative frequency of biblical references from the period."

[20]Bauckham, *Jesus and the Eyewitnesses*, 303.

provide us with a sound basis for investigating the historical question of what Jesus did, what he said, and who he claimed to be."[21]

It will also be helpful here to explore very briefly the backgrounds of the traditional authors. While two of them, Matthew and John, were considered eyewitnesses, the other two, Mark and Luke, were not. Instead, they were associated with the apostles. We learn in Matthew 10:3 that Matthew was a tax collector, and Irenaeus informs us that Matthew wrote his Gospel in the Hebrew dialect, something Papias claimed decades earlier (see Eusebius, *Ecclesiastical History* 3.39.15).[22] John was the "beloved disciple" who is frequently considered to be John the son of Zebedee. Mark was Peter's interpreter, something Papias reported decades earlier as well.[23] The Mark who is being referred to here is often believed to have been John Mark, mentioned throughout the New Testament (Acts 15:37; Col 4:10; 1 Pet 5:13). Luke was Paul's traveling companion, indicated by the various "we" passages in Acts (e.g., Acts 16:10-17).[24] His work is associated not only with Paul but also other witnesses (Lk 1:1-4).[25]

---

[21]Pitre, *Case for Jesus*, 101.

[22]Regarding Matthew, there are questions regarding whether he actually wrote in Hebrew or Greek, why he would use a source such as Mark if he was a witness, and others. For an example of scholars engaging in the depth of these issues, see W. D. Davies and Dale C. Allison Jr., *Matthew 1–7*, ICC 1 (Edinburgh: T&T Clark, 1988). One may be surprised to learn that scholars recognize that "at one level very little hangs on the question of the authorship of this gospel. By and large, neither its meaning nor its authority is greatly changed if one decides that its author was not an apostle" (Carson and Moo, *Introduction to the New Testament*, 150). See also Ben Witherington III, *Invitation to the New Testament: First Things*, 2nd ed. (New York: Oxford University Press, 2017), 252-53. Part of the reason for this, it might be suggested, is that eyewitness material has been found in the Gospels, as argued in Bauckham, *Jesus and the Eyewitnesses*.

[23]Papias comments, "Mark being the interpreter of Peter whatsoever he recorded he wrote with great accuracy but not however, in the order in which it was spoken or done by our Lord, for he neither heard nor followed our Lord, but as before said, he was in company with Peter" (Eusebius, *Ecclesiastical History* 3.39.15).

[24]Additionally, Luke seems an unlikely invention of the early church. As D. A. Carson and Douglas Moo point out, the "universal identification of a non-apostle as the author of almost one-quarter of the New Testament speaks strongly for the authenticity of the tradition" (*Introduction to the New Testament*, 206).

[25]Tertullian notes that not only was Luke Paul's traveling partner, but Marcion, the second-century heretic, "singled out Luke for his mutilating process" (Tertullian, *Against Marcion* 4.2). This indicates that even opponents of the church, such as Marcion, recognized Luke as the author.

These same four names are universally attested in the early church. There were no competing names, and it seems highly unlikely that these works circulated as genuinely anonymous works. As we will see in chapter eleven, the four Gospels were widely accepted as authoritative and included on various canonical lists. The names associated with these Gospels were well known from an early period without competitors.

KEY TAKEAWAYS: NEW TESTAMENT AUTHORSHIP

- In the New Testament, we have letters written by Paul, who was a persecutor of the church before converting to Christianity and preaching the message he had previously sought to destroy.
- There are thirteen letters that bear Paul's name. Of these letters, even critical skeptics accept seven as undisputedly Pauline letters.
- Though the Gospels are technically anonymous, it is unlikely that they were functionally anonymous and intended to be anonymous.
- There is an incredible consistency regarding the names associated with each of the Gospels, originating *early*. The *only* names associated with the four Gospels are Matthew, Mark, Luke, and John.

RECOMMENDED READING

Hengel, Martin. *The Four Gospels and the One Gospel of Jesus Christ: An Investigation of the Collection and Origin of the Canonical Gospels.* Translated by John Bowden. Harrisburg, PA: Trinity Press International, 2000.

Köstenberger, Andreas J., L. Scott Kellum, and Charles L. Quarles. *The Cradle, the Cross, and the Crown: An Introduction to the New Testament.* Nashville: B&H Academic, 2009.

Wright, N. T., and Michael F. Bird. *The New Testament in Its World: An Introduction to the History, Literature, and Theology of the First Christians.* Grand Rapids, MI: Zondervan Academic, 2019.

5

NEW TESTAMENT CREEDAL TRADITIONS

In this chapter I will present a unifying theme of the previous chapter by introducing New Testament creedal traditions. To recap, we have seen that the New Testament has the right words and suitable genres, and was written early and by relevant authors. As we will see, creeds combine these and other characteristics *with an even higher degree of reliability*. Due to their nature, the creeds help us to zoom in more closely on particular areas within the landscape presented in the New Testament.

When we hear of Christian creeds, we likely think of things such as the Apostles' Creed or Nicene Creed. Often various confessions are associated with creeds, and here we may be thinking of something such as the Westminster Confession of Faith. If you are not familiar with these, do not worry because *none* of these are the creeds or confessions I will discuss here. The focus of this chapter will be to introduce creeds found *within the New Testament*.

This chapter will introduce what I mean by New Testament creeds (or confessions, hymns, etc.). Given its popularity, I will use a widely accepted creed that begins at 1 Corinthians 15:3 as an example for our discussion. I will also highlight the *very early dating* of these creeds, since they *predate* the New Testament writings themselves. In so doing, I will also show how the apostles are connected to them before emphasizing the significance of these creeds.

INTRODUCTION TO CREEDS

If I am not referring to the Apostles' Creed or the Westminster Confession, what am I referring to? We can think of New Testament creeds as sources *within* sources. Similar to how one author may quote another writer's text, the New Testament quotes several very early oral traditions, also known as creeds, confessions, hymns, and so on. These are formalized statements circulated in the earliest period of Christianity and before any New Testament writing.

There are a variety of reasons that creeds developed. Oscar Cullmann believes there are at least five different reasons, each of which is *simultaneously* possible, for the development of these formulations in the first place: baptism/catechumenism, preaching/liturgy, exorcism, persecution, and polemics.[1] Other scholars have sought to differentiate between different formulations (hymns, creeds, confessions, etc.).[2] I want to note that throughout this chapter I will refer to the phenomenon using the catchall terms *creed* or *creedal traditions*.

In the ancient world, some could read, but many could not. For pragmatic reasons, the ancient world was in many ways an oral world. Having easily memorizable creeds would have been an effective way to pass on information. They could be created effectively in various ways, but a rough analogy familiar to many today is songs or poems. They have a rhythm and cadence that makes them more memorable. Many of us, for example, can still recall nursery rhymes or children's songs we learned (Jack and Jill, Mary Had a Little Lamb, etc.), or, if the marketing is good, we can recall jingles from different commercials we have seen or heard as well.

Of course, within ancient oral traditions in general and those found in the New Testament in particular, the topics were not merely

[1]Oscar Cullmann, *The Earliest Christian Confessions*, trans. J. K. S. Reid, ed. Gary Habermas and Benjamin Charles Shaw (repr., Eugene, OR: Wipf & Stock, 2018), 18.

[2]Almost a dozen different classifications are given in Richard N. Longenecker, "Christological Materials in the Early Christian Communities," in *Contours of Christology in the New Testament*, ed. Richard N. Longenecker (Grand Rapids, MI: Eerdmans, 2005), 69.

children's songs. Creedal formulas have certain features that made them distinctive. These elements have also allowed historians to better identify creedal formulas within the New Testament.

FIRST CORINTHIANS 15

The most explicit example of a creed, and perhaps the most studied, is the one beginning at 1 Corinthians 15:3 This creed is a particularly helpful example because Paul is explicit in introducing it. Let us look at the creed in 1 Corinthians 15 by first starting with 1 Corinthians 15:1-5:

> Now I make known to you, brothers and sisters, the gospel which I preached to you, which you also received, in which you also stand, by which you also are saved, if you hold firmly to the word which I preached to you, unless you believed in vain.
>
> For I handed down to you as of first importance what I also received, that Christ died for our sins according to the Scriptures, and that He was buried, and that he was raised on the third day according to the Scriptures, and that He appeared to Cephas, then to the twelve.

Many of us have likely read through 1 Corinthians 15 and overlooked the importance of these verses. Paul is providing several details relevant to our discussion on creeds.

First, he states that he is reminding them of the gospel he preached when he was with them. So this is not new information but what he already gave them at an earlier date. Moreover, it is central to the Christian message because Paul says that it is the "gospel" and by it "you also are saved." Indeed, it is of "first importance."

Paul is reminding (or "[re]deliver[ing]") the Corinthians of something he himself had "received." In the Greek, these are two technical words for the formal passing on of rabbinic traditions.[3] This makes sense not only because was Paul a Pharisee (Phil 3:5) but also because the first believers were Jewish. Accordingly, these words provide key

[3]Paul W. Barnett, *Jesus and the Logic of History* (Grand Rapids, MI: Eerdmans, 1997), 44-45.

indicators that Paul is getting ready to remind the Corinthians of a formal tradition he had received.

While there is some discussion on where the creed actually ends, it is widely agreed that it includes 1 Corinthians 15:3-5.[4] The verses, among other aspects, feature parallelism, a threefold "and that" wording, and words not typically used by Paul.[5] Thus, the "context and a certain rhythm allow us to discern the citation," and Paul's introductory comments explicitly state that a creed is used.[6] Accordingly, we can be confident about what a creed looks like here, which helps scholars identify other creeds when they are not so clearly identified (see below).

Where did Paul "receive" this creed? If this is an early creed, and Paul says he received it, where did it come from? Scholars have put forward a few options. Some think that after Paul's conversion, he was given various creeds in Damascus while spending time with other disciples (Acts 9:10-22). Some think that perhaps Paul heard some creeds while he was persecuting the church—after all, Paul had to have some idea of the people he was persecuting and what they believed. Another option is that Paul received it in Jerusalem.

Many, including skeptics, think the Jerusalem option to be the best because of Paul's comments in Galatians 1–2. Specifically, in Galatians 1:18-19 Paul says, "Then three years later [after Paul's conversion] I went up to Jerusalem to become acquainted [*historēsai*] with Cephas, and stayed with him fifteen days. But I did not see another one of the apostles except James, the Lord's brother."

Paul informs us that shortly after his conversion, which was around AD 32, he went to Jerusalem and met Peter and James.

[4]"This does not affect the basic point to be made. . . . What counts is the heart of the formula is something Paul knows the Corinthians will have heard from everyone else as well as himself, and that he can appeal to it as unalterable Christian bedrock." N. T. Wright, *The Resurrection of the Son of God*, Christian Origins and the Question of God 3 (Minneapolis: Fortress, 2003), 319.

[5]For a brief summary of eight reasons, see Pinchas Lapide, *The Resurrection of Jesus: A Jewish Perspective* (Eugene, OR: Wipf & Stock, 2002), 98-99. For a more extensive list, see Longenecker, "Christological Materials," 69-71.

[6]Cullmann, *Earliest Christian Confessions*, 20n1

Biblical scholar C. H. Dodd famously said, "At that time, he stayed with Peter for a fortnight, and we may presume they did not spend all the time talking about the weather."[7] Even if Paul did not receive the creed here, the content of it would have undoubtedly been confirmed by two "pillars" of the church, Peter and James (Gal 2:9). The context of both Galatians 1 and 1 Corinthians 15 is the gospel, which is, after all, of "first importance."

So there is Paul, just a few years after his conversion, meeting with a leading disciple and Jesus' brother. But there is more. In Galatians 2:1-10, Paul writes that he made another trip to Jerusalem fourteen years later. This time, in addition to Peter and James, John was there. The reported "pillars" of the church gave Paul "the right hand of fellowship" (Gal 2:9). Paul's gospel message that was of "first importance" was confirmed a second time. It seems highly unlikely that Peter, James, and John would have given the right hand of fellowship to a heretic preaching a false gospel. Moreover, in 1 Corinthians 15:11, Paul states that the gospel message he preaches is the same message as that of the church ("so we preach and so you believed").

When was this creed developed? Earlier I presented a general timeline that began with Jesus' death, around AD 30. We may add to that timeline Paul's first visit to Corinth, around AD 50, and his letter to them (1 Corinthians), dated to around AD 55. More importantly, Paul's conversion, around AD 32, is included, along with his first trip to Jerusalem about three years later, around AD 35. Of course, while some people knew the creed before Paul's conversion, at the very least those who gave the creed to Paul had to know it *before delivering it to him* (whether in Damascus or Jerusalem). Last, I have included Paul's second trip to Jerusalem as well.

[7]C. H. Dodd, *The Apostolic Preaching and Its Developments* (New York: Harper & Row, 1964), 16. Similarly, the agnostic Ehrman writes, "It defies belief that Paul would have spent over two weeks with Jesus's closest companion and not learned something about him." Bart D. Ehrman, *Did Jesus Exist? The Historical Argument for Jesus of Nazareth* (New York: HarperOne, 2012), 145.

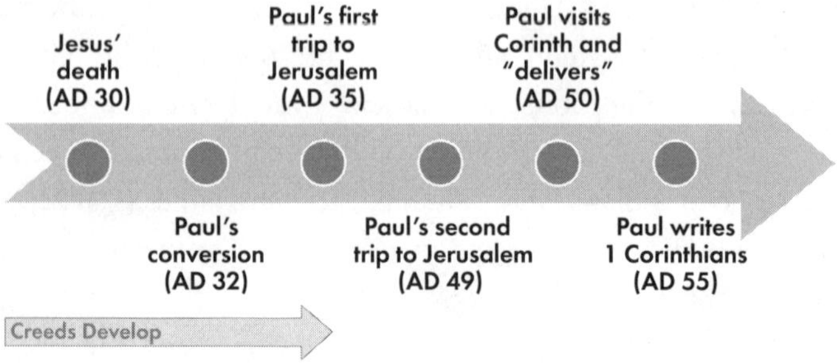

Figure 5.1. When the creeds developed

Accordingly, virtually all scholars date this and other creeds *to the early 30s AD*. In a recent study on 1 Corinthians 15, James Ware states, "There is almost universal scholarly consensus that 1 Cor 15.3–5 contains a carefully preserved tradition pre-dating Paul's apostolic activity and *received* by him within two to five years of the founding events."[8]

The "almost universal" consensus includes skeptical scholars. For example, atheist New Testament scholar Gerd Lüdemann writes, "*The formation of the appearance traditions mentioned in 1 Cor. 15.3-8 falls into the time between 30 and 33 CE*."[9] Similarly, skeptic Bart Ehrman agrees that the traditions Paul received in Jerusalem "must date to just a couple of years after Jesus's death."[10] Just as Paul delivered the creed to the Corinthians, so too it must have been delivered to Paul as a tradition that existed before it was also received by Paul.

In short, if Paul *received* the material around AD 35, or three years after his conversion, the material *delivered* to him must have existed before then. The late James Dunn asserts that we can be "entirely confident" the creedal information in 1 Corinthians 15 was "*formulated as*

[8]James Ware, "The Resurrection of Jesus in the Pre-Pauline Formula of 1 Cor 15.3-5," *New Testament Studies* 60, no. 4 (2014): 475, emphasis added.

[9]Gerd Lüdemann, *The Resurrection of Jesus: History, Experience, Theology*, trans. John Bowden (Minneapolis: Fortress, 1994), 38, emphasis original. For a list of other skeptical scholars who follow similar dating, see Gary R. Habermas, *The Risen Jesus and Future Hope* (Lanham, MD: Rowman & Littlefield, 2003), 18.

[10]Ehrman, *Did Jesus Exist?*, 131; see also 164, 251, 254. Ehrman notes the early date of this material and Paul's trip to Jerusalem (130-32, 144-48, 155-56, 173, 261).

tradition within months of Jesus' death."[11] It would have been formulated while Paul was a persecutor of the church and, as Dunn notes, would have been developed as the apostles began sharing the gospel.

EARLY EYEWITNESS TESTIMONY

Let me take a moment to summarize what I have so quickly introduced. In part, the early church used creeds as condensed versions of larger narratives about Jesus and the gospel. In the case of 1 Corinthians 15:3-8 we saw an explicit reference to a creed as of "first importance," and it refers to Jesus' death, burial, and appearances.

Paul gave the creed to the Corinthians around AD 50, while he received it himself in the early 30s AD. At the very least, the information would have been confirmed by leaders of the Jerusalem church three years after his conversion (Gal 1:18). Yet it would have existed prior to his conversion. This series of events carries great significance because it greatly adds to the reliability of this creedal information.

For example, regarding Paul's first meeting with Peter and James, Ehrman writes, "These are two good people to know if you want to know anything about the historical Jesus. I wish I knew them." He then asks, "Can we get any closer to an eyewitness report than this?"[12] More forcefully, Jewish scholar Pinchas Lapide concludes, "This unified piece of tradition which soon was solidified into a formula of faith may be considered as a statement of eyewitnesses for whom the experience of the resurrection became the turning point of their lives."[13] Similarly, Richard Bauckham stresses that this is "*eyewitness testimony* of those who were recipients of resurrection appearances, including the most prominent in the Jerusalem church."[14]

The connection of the eyewitnesses to the creeds is robust, as these three scholars recognize it despite their having different theological

[11]James D. G. Dunn, *Jesus Remembered* (Grand Rapids, MI: Eerdmans, 2003), 1:855, emphasis original.

[12]Ehrman, *Did Jesus Exist?*, 144-45; see also 146-48.

[13]Lapide, *Resurrection of Jesus*, 99.

[14]Richard Bauckham, *Jesus and the Eyewitnesses: The Gospels as Eyewitness Testimony* (Grand Rapids, MI: Eerdmans, 2006), 308, emphasis original.

backgrounds. There is good reason for this. Paul, himself an eyewitness and important figure in early Christianity, says directly that he met and spoke with the "pillars" of the Jerusalem church on more than one occasion. Accordingly, the connection to the eyewitnesses regarding this information has considerable historical weight.

The situation is similar for the dating of the creed, as the early dating of the creed is also widely accepted. This reporting close to the time of the events involved adds historical weight to these claims. Moreover, these creedal statements provide insight into the earliest Christian reports, which occurred even *prior* to Paul's writing.

OTHER CREEDS

The creed beginning at 1 Corinthians 15:3 was our test case because Paul explicitly refers to a tradition. The situation is similar regarding the other creeds within the New Testament. Paul's first trip to Jerusalem is "most likely" the place where he learned many of the creeds we see in his writings, according to Ehrman. He writes, "This visit is one of the *most likely* places where Paul learned all the received traditions that he refers to and even the received traditions that we otherwise suspect are in his writings that he does not name as such."[15] Thus, it is *not* just the creed in 1 Corinthians 15 but other traditions that Paul likely received during this early trip to Jerusalem, and consequently, as widely recognized, these creeds typically date to the 30s AD.

Some other creedal formulations include critical christological texts such as Romans 1:3-4; Romans 10:9; Philippians 2:6-11; 1 Corinthians 8:6. As with the creed in 1 Corinthians 15, these creedal statements are specific and central claims to earliest Christianity. It is highly unlikely Paul could have met with Peter and James while preaching a message that was at odds with theirs. Furthermore, in the second meeting, where John was also present, all three gave Paul (and Barnabas) the right hand of fellowship.

[15]Ehrman, *Did Jesus Exist?*, 131. Similar comments can be found regarding multiple traditions dating to the 30s on 92-93, 97, 141, 251, 260-63. Emphasis added.

Early oral formulas are also thought to be found in other New Testament writings.[16] Notable examples are located in the speeches and sermon summaries throughout the book of Acts. Hebrews 4:14 and 1 Peter 2:22-23 are other examples. Some scholars suggest there may be as many as forty or fifty creeds within the New Testament and that they vary from short one-liners to a few verses long.[17]

CONCLUSION

There are several evidential considerations here that add to the case for the reliability of the New Testament. In the case of the creeds found in Paul's writings, we have powerful historical considerations featuring both eyewitness and early historical information. First, these creeds and Paul's trip to Jerusalem are reported in "undisputed" Pauline works (1 Corinthians and Galatians). Second, just three years after Paul's conversion, he met with James and Peter in Jerusalem to "inquire" with them.[18] Fourteen years later, he met them again, along with John, before he was given the right hand of fellowship. Third, the creedal information in 1 Corinthians 15 is said to be central to the gospel and of "first importance." It is unlikely that the "pillars" would have approved of someone who got the core of the gospel wrong. Having reports that are dated very close to the events and connected to eyewitnesses is valuable to historians precisely because it is reliable data.

KEY TAKEAWAYS: NEW TESTAMENT CREEDAL TRADITIONS

- There are many creedal traditions in the New Testament. These creeds reflect oral traditions that existed prior to the writing of the New Testament itself.

---

[16]Vernon H. Neufeld, *The Earliest Christian Confessions*, New Testament Tools and Studies 5 (Grand Rapids, MI: Eerdmans, 1963).

[17]Longenecker, "Christological Materials," 71.

[18]One might add another level of reliability here in that Peter, James, and Paul were all willing to suffer and die for their beliefs.

- It is widely accepted by scholars that traditions that Paul cites likely go back to around the 30s AD. We know that Paul met with two major figures of Christianity, Peter and James, in Galatians 1–2.
- One of the best and earliest creeds in the New Testament is the one beginning in 1 Corinthians 15:3. This tradition is connected with eyewitnesses such as Peter, James, and Paul. It is also considered to be the earliest historical evidence for Jesus' resurrection, since it predates the Gospels and Paul's writings.

RECOMMENDED READING

Cullmann, Oscar. *The Earliest Christian Confessions*. Translated by J. K. S. Reid. Edited by Gary Habermas and Benjamin Charles Shaw. Reprint, Eugene, OR: Wipf & Stock, 2018.

Dodd, C. H. *The Apostolic Preaching and Its Developments*. New York: Harper & Row, 1964.

Neufeld, Vernon H. *The Earliest Christian Confessions*. New Testament Tools and Studies 5. Grand Rapids, MI: Eerdmans, 1963.

6

HISTORICAL CRITERIA

In the introduction, I framed this project as analogous to Google Maps in some ways. The previous chapters gave us primarily zoomed-out perspectives and helped us know which country we were examining. Now I will zoom in and observe some of the various states, cities, and streets. In other words, the textual evidence, genre, dating, creeds, and authorship of the various New Testament books provide reasonable grounds for thinking these texts are generally reliable as well as some specifics (e.g., the creedal information in 1 Cor 15). I will continue to zoom in on some more particulars. There are historical criteria that historians use in order to better determine the probability of various events reported in the New Testament.

AN OVERVIEW

What are these criteria, and how are they applied? Consider for a moment the following story. Imagine that you are a detective and have encountered a scene where two teenage drivers were in a car accident. One drives a silver car and the other a blue car. How would you go about finding out who was at fault in the accident if there are no video recordings? What are the sorts of things you would want to know?

Initially, getting statements from each driver would be a good place to start. Because of their biases and self-interest, you might expect that each driver will say that they were innocent and that the other person was guilty. Of course, they cannot both be right.

Next, you will want to try to see whether there were any witnesses to the incident. Perhaps there were people nearby who observed the crash. You can ask these witnesses what happened and see what they report. If these witnesses report that the "light," "gray," or "silver" car did not stop and crashed into the "dark" or "blue" car, then you begin to have some positive reasons to believe that this was in fact the case.

I should note here that these witnesses need to be *independent witnesses*. If one person tells five others, then there is only one witness, not six. Repeats and retweets do not count. The more independent witnesses you have, the higher the probability that the silver car crashed into the blue car because it failed to stop.

In addition to these witnesses, a passenger was in the silver car and gives their statement. This passenger also happens to be the father of the driver. You think that his testimony is also important and ask him what happened. He responds, "My son was not paying attention and drove through the stop sign without stopping." This would be strong evidence for the guilt of the driver of the silver car because his own father is providing *embarrassing information*. Specifically, that his son was the guilty driver.

Last, you find out that one of the earlier witnesses is currently involved in a court case against the driver of the blue car. However, this witness testified that it was not the blue car that caused the accident but the silver car. This witness acknowledged the innocence of their otherwise legal *opponent*.

Each of these different factors adds to the probability that, in fact, the silver car was at fault. This is because there are *multiple independent witnesses, embarrassing testimony, and enemy attestation*. While these criteria do not give us certainty (nothing in history is 100 percent certain), they help to move us from the merely possible to the more (and more) probable.

While this is just an introductory example, we can begin to see the ways we usually think about the past presented more explicitly. The different criteria reflect various intuitions and differences that are often taken for granted. With this in mind, it is important to note that these criteria are not like mathematical laws. We cannot simply expect to plug the criteria into a formula and then simply get the conclusion. Instead, the criteria are more like proverbs to be applied at the proper time. Knowing when to apply "Look before you leap" and "He who hesitates is lost" will depend on various factors.[1] In our context, they will be considered part of a larger historical argument. Moreover, we need to note that these criteria typically only add to the probability of a past event. The more criteria are met, the more likely an event has occurred, but their absence does not argue against an event.

When it comes to the New Testament, some standard criteria are frequently used. Here are some of the more common examples:

- ***Reported early:*** Events that are reported shortly after an event are preferred over those that are reported later. As we saw in previous chapters, not only are the dates for various New Testament writings considered to be within the lifetime of the eyewitnesses, but within Paul's own early writings are Christian creeds that are dated *very* early.
- ***Multiple independent attestation:*** This criterion obtains when an event is reported by multiple sources that are not dependent on one another. This is perhaps the most popular criterion used by scholars, especially because many reports in ancient history are found in only one literary source. It is important to remember that the New Testament is not just one book but a collection of writings from different authors. Note that if an account is found in the Synoptic Gospels, then it is typically deemed one source because most scholars believe Matthew and Luke used Mark as a source. Thus, if Matthew and Luke report something found in Mark, it is usually considered to be one source: Mark.
- ***Multiple forms:*** Reports found in different forms, such as narratives, parables, creedal statements, and so on, are likely to be earlier and thus more reliable. An example of an event meeting this criterion would be Jesus' burial, as it is found in both the

[1]Ben Meyer helpfully provides this clarification. See Meyer, *Critical Realism and the New Testament* (Allison Park, PA: Wipf & Stock, 1989), 141.

creed of 1 Corinthians 15:4 and the narratives of the Gospels and elsewhere (e.g., Rom 6:4).

- ***Embarrassing testimony:*** When a source admits to an event understood as an embarrassing admission, it adds to the probability that the event occurred. A notable example of embarrassing testimony in the New Testament is found in Jesus' reference to Peter's denial of him, which is undoubtedly not something one would invent about the leader of the early church. Further, the embarrassing nature of Jesus' death by crucifixion is hard to overstate (as even Paul notes in 1 Cor 1:23).
- ***Enemy/disinterested attestation:*** If a rival source concedes some information favorable to their opponent, it adds to the likeliness of this information being accurate.[2] Enemies or disinterested sources are not likely to offer up positive data unless they agree it is accurate, and they may nevertheless describe it in a negative light.
- ***Consistency/coherence:*** This is one of the few criteria with a negative function in that if it is not met, the event in question is deemed *less likely*. This criterion requires that an event coheres with what we know of the historical context in which it is situated. When it comes to the New Testament, if a text were to report the disciples riding motorcycles to get from one town to the next, then it would fail to cohere with what we know about the first century.

Now that I have given a brief overview of these criteria, how can they be applied to questions of the historical reliability of the New Testament? They can be used in establishing both various themes, such as Jesus as a miracle worker, and specific claims, such as Jesus predicting his death and resurrection. Below I will briefly examine these claims and show how historical criteria help to establish them.[3]

---

[2]Related to this are disinterested sources that have no vested interest in the outcome of an event.

[3]In the final chapter, I will discuss these criteria in relation to events surrounding Jesus' death and resurrection.

JESUS AS A MIRACLE WORKER

As I noted above, historical criteria can add probability that a reported event occurred but are only part of an overall argument. The goal here is to illustrate how various historical criteria can be applied to New Testament claims. There are several other arguments for Jesus as a miracle worker, and what is presented below should not be considered exhaustive.[4] The aim here is to highlight how these criteria apply to the New Testament claims.

- ***Multiple attestation:*** Reports about Jesus' miracles are found in a significant number of texts. They are found not only throughout the New Testament writings (Gospels, Acts, epistles, Revelation) but also in non-Christian sources (Josephus, rabbinic traditions, Celsus). Each of these sources, from varying perspectives, acknowledges that Jesus performed wondrous works.
- ***Enemy attestation:*** Not all of the reports are charitable toward Jesus. For example, in the Gospels, the Pharisees do not attempt to explain away the event but rather state that Jesus' works are done by the power of "Beelzebul the ruler of the demons" (Mt 12:24; see also Mt 9:34; Mk 3:22; Lk 11:15). Though the rabbinic traditions found in the Talmud are later, they are consistent with Pharisaic claims found the Gospels that attribute the actions of Jesus to "sorcery" (Sanhedrin 43a). The third-century theologian Origen reports that a critic of Christianity named Celsus raised similar accusations against Jesus (Origen, *Contra Celsus* 2.49-50). Around the end of the first century, Jewish historian Josephus reports that Jesus was a "doer of wonderful works" (Josephus, *Antiquities of the Jews* 18.3).[5] These sources provide data that others in the ancient

[4]Graham H. Twelftree, *Jesus the Miracle Worker: A Historical and Theological Study* (Downers Grove, IL: IVP Academic, 1999); Twelftree, "The Miracles of Jesus: Marginal or Mainstream?," *Journal for the Study of the Historical Jesus* 1, no. 1 (January 2003): 104-24. See also Michael R. Licona, *The Resurrection of Jesus: A New Historiographical Approach* (Downers Grove, IL: IVP Academic, 2010), 281-83.

[5]It should be noted that this comment comes in a questioned portion of Josephus's text. Nevertheless, scholars such as James D. G. Dunn find it relevant here. See James K. Beilby

world believed Jesus did *something* but try to explain this *something* in terms of wickedness rather than beneficence.

- ***Embarrassing testimony:*** There is also embarrassing testimony regarding the miracles of Jesus. In Mark 6:1-6 (and Mt 13:57-58) Jesus performs fewer miracles because of the unbelief that was present. This is hardly something one would expect Mark to invent! We also see in Matthew 11:20; 21:32 that Jesus rebukes those who saw the miracles but did not repent afterward (see Lk 10:13-16). These are not the types of things one would want to include unless they were known.
- ***Reported early:*** A final consideration here is the early nature of these miracle reports. They are found throughout the Gospels, including the Gospel of Mark. They are also located in the early material of the Acts sermon summaries (which likely predate the Gospels). Peter, for example, in Acts 2:22 refers to the miracles performed by Jesus, as he does again in Acts 10:37-39. The material in these sermon summaries is often dated very early and likely predates the Gospels.[6]

Recall the example above regarding a car accident. The same *principles* apply here. Each of these criteria adds to the historical weight that Jesus was in fact a miracle worker. The case is so strong that the late Marcus Borg argues, "Despite the difficulty which miracles pose for the modern mind, on historical grounds it is virtually indisputable that Jesus was a healer and exorcist."[7] We ought to remember, however, that we were not trying to make the entire historical case here, nor should we think these criteria are all we need. There are other historical considerations. Nevertheless, the criteria provide important factors regarding the historicity of all reported events, and this includes Jesus' being a miracle worker or our example of a car accident. The words of

---

and Paul R. Eddy, *The Historical Jesus: Five Views* (Downers Grove, IL: IVP Academic, 2009), 222 (Dunn). I will discuss this more in chapter nine.

[6]See chapter five.

[7]Marcus J. Borg, *Jesus: A New Vision—Spirit, Culture, and the Life of Discipleship* (New York: Harper & Row, 1987), 61.

Graham Twelftree are significant in this regard when he writes, "We have seen that it is not a matter of so-called blind faith that enables us to say this."[8] Indeed!

JESUS' PREDICTING HIS DEATH AND RESURRECTION

While Jesus' predictions are discussed in detail elsewhere, I will briefly summarize four criteria and how they apply to the claim that Jesus predicted his death and resurrection.[9] Again, this should not be considered an exhaustive list but a sample of how the criteria are applied to the claims of the New Testament.

- ***Multiple attestation:*** Jesus' predictions are multiply attested in different sources. For example, Jesus tells the disciples about his impending death and resurrection, leading Peter to rebuke Jesus. Jesus' response to this is to rebuke Peter by saying, "Get behind Me, Satan." This account is found in Mark 8:31-33 and Matthew 16:21-23, while Luke 9:22 has the prediction only. When an event is found in Mark, Matthew, and Luke (the Synoptics), it is typically considered to be only one source.[10] However, this appears to be one of those few instances where Matthew and Luke do *not* appear to be dependent on Mark, and thus it satisfies multiple attestation.[11] Another relevant example here is the establishing of the Lord's Supper as reported in Mark 14:22-25; Matthew 26:26-29; Luke 22:19-20; and, importantly, in a pre-Pauline creed found in 1 Corinthians 11:24-25. Regarding the Lord's Supper, the

---

[8]Twelftree, *Jesus the Miracle Worker*, 345.

[9]Licona, *Resurrection of Jesus*, 284-302; Michael Licona, "Did Jesus Predict His Death and Vindication/Resurrection?," *Journal for the Study of the Historical Jesus* 8, no. 1 (2010): 47-66. Even skeptical scholars are willing to accept this fact without assigning the cause to divine agency. Rather, they affirm Jesus' wisdom to recognize what would likely happen as a result of challenging the Jewish authorities.

[10]The reason for this is that the majority of scholars hold that Mark wrote first and Matthew and Luke used Mark as one of their sources. Thus, if Mark reports an event and Matthew and Luke merely copy Mark, it only counts as one source. In modern terms, retweets do not count. One must be careful concerning the use of multiple attestation with Matthew, Mark, and Luke.

[11]For more details see Licona, *Resurrection of Jesus*, 285.

creedal material is the earliest, and additional corroboration of this event is found in Mark.

- ***Multiple forms:*** We have already alluded to the fact that Jesus' impending death and resurrection were predicted in multiple forms, since they are mentioned in the Gospel narratives and in the creedal material of 1 Corinthians 11:24-25. While there are narrative accounts of Jesus making these predictions, there are also parables, such as the parable of the wicked tenants (Mk 12:1-12). The sign of Jonah (Mt 12:38-40) is another example. We thus find reports of these predictions in a multitude of forms (narratives, creeds, parables, etc.).[12]
- ***Reported early:*** Events found in multiple forms, such as those mentioned, are considered to be early. In addition, we find the creedal material in Paul referencing the Last Supper. Of course, it is also found in the earliest Gospel, Mark.
- ***Embarrassing testimony:*** While Peter's rebuke of Jesus may be considered embarrassing (Mk 8:32), Jesus' referring to Peter as Satan certainly is (Mk 8:33)! This is all the more embarrassing since Peter became one of the "pillars" of the early church (Gal 2:9) and this account is included in Mark, who is often believed to have been Peter's interpreter. It is not something he would have been likely to make up. Additionally, the manner of Jesus' death is highly embarrassing (1 Cor 1:23), and some find Jesus' prayer in the garden before the crucifixion disconcerting (Mk 14:32-41).

As with our previous example, these four criteria illustrate how historians can assess the reports we have. Each of these criteria, and others, contributes to the case that Jesus' death and resurrection were likely predicted ahead of time. The criteria used here parallel the analysis we would use regarding other claims about the past.

[12]The list here should not be understood to be exhaustive.

CONCLUSION

We must remember that the Bible is a collection of writings from different authors. Significantly, even those who think the Bible is *unreliable* will use these historical criteria to ferret out what they believe to be *reliable* information.[13] Historians do not depend on reports to be wholly accurate in order to make accurate judgments about the past. There are a number of historically unreliable texts—past and present—from which we can still discern reliable historical data by using these criteria.[14] They thus provide unique and helpful tools in showing specific (zoomed-in) reports of the New Testament to be reliable, such as the two examples I briefly highlighted (see chapter thirteen for another example regarding Jesus' death).

KEY TAKEAWAYS

- The historical criteria discussed here are intuitive and used today regarding current events. Historical criteria are typically used to add probability to the historicity of an event. These criteria can be applied to reports to better discern whether an event occurred.
- The criteria can be effectively applied to sources that are considered reliable or unreliable.
- These criteria can be applied to the New Testament, and when they are, they yield strong weight to the historicity of various reported events (e.g., Jesus' predictions).

RECOMMENDED READING

Bock, Darrell L., and J. Ed Komoszewski, eds. *Jesus, Skepticism and the Problem of History: Criteria and Context in the Study of Christian Origins*. Grand Rapids, MI: Zondervan Academic, 2019.

---

[13]Atheist/agnostic Bart Ehrman is a good example. See Bart D. Ehrman, *How Jesus Became God: The Exaltation of a Jewish Preacher from Galilee* (New York: HarperOne, 2014), 94.

[14]See, for example, the list of historical facts provided in Robert M. Bowman Jr. and J. Ed Komoszewski, "The Historical Jesus and the Biblical Church: Why the Quest Matters," in *Jesus, Skepticism and the Problem of History: Criteria and Context in the Study of Christian Origins*, ed. Darrell L. Bock and J. Ed Komoszewski (Grand Rapids, MI: Zondervan Academic, 2019), 22-23.

Burr, Kevin B. *Authenticating Criteria in Jesus Research and Beyond: An Interdisciplinary Methodology*. Biblical Interpretation Series 219. Leiden: Brill, 2023.

Charlesworth, James H. *The Historical Jesus: An Essential Guide*. Nashville: Abingdon, 2008.

7

UNDESIGNED COINCIDENCES

Undesigned coincidences have not typically been present in discussions on New Testament reliability even though they have been recognized for years. One of the first publications that focused strictly on undesigned coincidences was by J. J. Blunt in 1847, titled *Undesigned Coincidences in the Writings Both of the Old and New Testament: An Argument of Their Veracity*.[1] However, undesigned coincidences have recently garnered more and more attention in reliability discussions. They can indeed be a helpful factor to consider because they address issues of reliability from a different angle from any of the ones mentioned thus far. The goal in this chapter is to introduce undesigned coincidences and provide some examples of how they corroborate New Testament accounts.

Before I do this, it is worth noting that undesigned coincidences generally provide zoomed-in reliability perspectives.[2] The reason for this is because they corroborate events that are often isolated to a specific event. However, if a cumulative case is made and a number of undesigned coincidences are found within a writing, this would demonstrate that the author has consistently been reliable at various points. If an author has been reliable where we can verify, then it

---

[1]J. J. Blunt, *Undesigned Coincidences in the Writings Both of the Old and New Testament: An Argument of Their Veracity* (New York: Robert Carter, 1847).

[2]Lydia McGrew, *Hidden in Plain View: Undesigned Coincidences in the Gospels and Acts* (Chillicothe, OH: DeWard, 2017), 13.

becomes reasonable to trust the same author in areas where we might not be able to corroborate the accounts. Or, in the words of F. F. Bruce, "Accuracy is a habit of mind, and we know from happy (or unhappy) experiences that some people are habitually accurate just as others can be depended upon to be inaccurate."[3]

INTRODUCING UNDESIGNED COINCIDENCES

So what is an undesigned coincidence? In a recent work on the subject, Lydia McGrew defines them this way: "An undesigned coincidence is a notable connection between two or more accounts or texts that doesn't seem to have been planned by the person or people giving the accounts. Despite their apparent independence, the items fit together like pieces of a puzzle."[4] The puzzle analogy is particularly helpful. Just as two puzzle pieces connect and bring clarity to the bigger picture, so too do undesigned coincidences bring clarity to the bigger picture of a historical report.[5]

European scholar Peter J. Williams describes them as an agreement between sources of such a kind that renders it "hard to imagine as deliberately contrived by either author to make the story look authentic. Often the agreement is so subtle and indirect that all but the most careful reader are likely to miss it."[6] The result is that an event reported by sources is considered more likely to be historical because the sources unintentionally corroborate one another.

The reason that undesigned coincidences add to the historical weight of a report is that if an event were fabricated or invented, then it is highly unlikely that there would be an actual coincidence between the two accounts. This is all the more the case when the data or events

---

[3]F. F. Bruce, *The New Testament Documents: Are They Reliable?*, 6th ed. (Grand Rapids, MI: Eerdmans, 1981), 91. This applies to other areas of reliability as well.

[4]McGrew, *Hidden in Plain View*, 12.

[5]Historians sometimes refer to this as illumination. See Michael R. Licona, *The Resurrection of Jesus: A New Historiographical Approach* (Downers Grove, IL: IVP Academic, 2010), 111. One need not concern oneself here with various nuances that can be made regarding the differences between an undesigned coincidence, illumination, etc. One can be content here with a general idea of how a bigger picture is presented.

[6]Peter J. Williams, *Can We Trust the Gospels?* (Wheaton, IL: Crossway, 2018), 87.

in question are of secondary importance. Details like this are often included when two different sources write about the same event but with different aims and points of emphasis.

Think of it this way. Imagine you are sharing a story with one of your friends about a car accident you were recently involved in. As you share your story, another passenger in the car comes along and shares many different but *complementary* details. Now, if one or both of you were inventing details wholesale, what are the odds that there would be any illumination of secondary or tertiary elements? Not very likely, indeed. Thus, as McGrew points out, "Casual comments, allusions, and omissions that *fit together* are not what one would find in different fictional or fictionalized works written by different people. They are also not to be expected among different legendary stories that grew up gradually long after the events. They *are* the sort of thing that one gets in real witness testimony from people close-up to real events."[7]

It is important to note that a single undesigned coincidence would not typically provide a knock-down argument. Instead, undesigned coincidences function best as part of a cumulative case where multiple examples are presented, with the weight of each one adding more and more to the overall argument. Each case will vary in its persuasiveness and effectiveness, with some examples being stronger than others. With this in mind, I can present only three cases here, though several others can be found in the recommended readings below.

WHAT DID HEROD SAY? MATTHEW AND LUKE EXPLAIN

Matthew 14:1-2 says that the words and deeds of Jesus reached Herod.[8] As Herod "heard the news about Jesus," his response to these reports was, "This is John the Baptist; he himself has been raised from the dead,

---

[7]McGrew, *Hidden in Plain View*, 15, emphasis original. She then goes on to cite the work of a cold-case detective, J. Warner Wallace, *Cold-Case Christianity: A Homicide Detective Investigates the Claims of the Gospels* (Colorado Springs: David C. Cook, 2013). See also Craig L. Blomberg, *The Historical Reliability of the New Testament: Countering the Challenges to Evangelical Christian Beliefs*, B&H Studies in Christian Apologetics (Nashville: B&H Academic, 2016), 273.

[8]This is referring to Herod Antipas, the tetrarch, who was the son of Herod the Great.

and that is why miraculous powers are at work in him."[9] What is interesting about these two verses is that they state that Herod said these comments *to his servants*.[10] This leads us to ask, How could Matthew have known these details if Herod reported them to his servants?

One could assume that Herod heard about Jesus from his servants and so his initial reply was to the very servants who told him about Jesus in the first place. This is possible, and if we had nothing else to go on, this would make logical sense of the text.[11] But it raises the question of how Matthew knew what Herod was talking about on *any* occasion, let alone a discussion that specifically mentions Jesus.[12]

Luke 8:1-3 provides a detail that some, such as McGrew, consider evidence of an undesigned coincidence with the text in Matthew. Luke's text states that there were some women who were following Jesus. One of these women was "Joanna the wife of Chuza, Herod's steward" (Lk 8:3). The wife of Herod's manager, then, was traveling with Jesus along with the Twelve. In addition to her mere presence, she is mentioned with others "who were contributing to their support out of their private means" (Lk 8:3).

Luke thus provides information about those close to Herod in an entirely different context. The result is that Luke and Matthew illuminate each other in ways that seem *highly unlikely* to have been contrived in advance. Matthew is the only one to reference Herod's discussion with his servants, while Luke mentions that the wife of Herod's manager traveled with Jesus, the Twelve, and many others. It seems incredible to suggest that Luke would have invented his text in order to explain Matthew's passing comment. Similarly, Matthew does not provide any evidence that he invented his text as a consequence of

[9]It is highly unlikely that Herod had any type of reincarnation in mind here.

[10]In Mk 6:14-16 and Lk 9:7-9, there is no mention of the servants.

[11]One should note, however, that people in the past, just like today, do not always act logically. Fears, desires, and so on can play a factor in decisions. See the notable but comical example made by C. S. Lewis regarding fears before a surgery in *Mere Christianity*, in *The Complete C. S. Lewis Signature Classics* (New York: HarperOne, 2007), 115-16.

[12]A point observed by McGrew in her treatment of this coincidence (which she attributes to Blunt; *Hidden in Plain View*, 87-89).

Luke 8:1-3.[13] The result is that these texts illuminate each other in a way that adds reliability to their reports.

WHY WOULD PHILIP KNOW? LUKE AND JOHN EXPLAIN

In John 6, readers are presented with an account of Jesus' feeding of the five thousand. One interesting component of John's report is that Jesus asks Philip where to purchase bread so they can buy food for the people to eat. In the Synoptic Gospels, a more general picture is presented, with the disciples responding to this issue as a group, but in John readers are given specifics. In John, Philip specifically is identified, is asked, and answers (Jn 6:5-7).

A few chapters earlier, readers were informed, "Philip was from Bethsaida, the city of Andrew and Peter" (Jn 1:44). So these three are all from the same town. So what? What does this have to do with John 6 and the feeding of five thousand or Jesus' querying Philip? These are good questions, and this information alone leaves these questions unanswered.

However, the Gospel of Luke makes an interesting comment that illuminates these texts. In Luke 9:10, readers are informed that the feeding of the five thousand occurred in Bethsaida. According to John, this is the town that Philip was from. Luke's text does not mention that Philip is from Bethsaida, so it is highly improbable that Luke invented Bethsaida as the location of the feeding in order to explain why Jesus asks Philip where to get food in John 6:5.

We might add to this the fact that both Andrew and Peter are also reportedly from Bethsaida, and neither of these two is asked where to get food. One would expect that if John were inventing this report, he would have had Jesus ask Peter where to get the food. Or he could have given a more general description like that found in the Synoptics. Yet this is *not* what we find. Rather, this undesigned coincidence between these two texts indicates reliability in their reports.

---

[13]One should note, however, that there are other references to those who are related to the house of Herod that could be relevant in a more detailed discussion (see Acts 13:1).

PROCONSULS? LUKE AND TACITUS EXPLAIN

The two previous examples use writings from the New Testament. While this is perfectly legitimate, I do want to present a possible example of how a source *outside* the New Testament could provide similar corroboration of a New Testament report. We should note, however, that this case is not as strong as the prior two.

In this example, the two sources are Acts, written by Luke, and the *Annals*, written by the Roman historian Tacitus.[14] In Acts 19:35-40, a riot is breaking out in Ephesus. The city clerk reminds the crowd in Acts 19:38 that if one wants to make a complaint, then "the courts are in session and proconsuls are available." (A proconsul was a Roman authority to whom a complaint could be taken.) The key feature here is that Luke uses the *plural*. This is crucial because it was an "elementary and universally known fact" that there was only *one* proconsul and not multiple proconsuls.[15]

As Craig Keener points out in his massive four-volume commentary on Acts, "It is next to impossible that Luke, as an urban citizen of the Roman Empire, was unaware that Rome assigned only one proconsul per province."[16] So, again, why does Luke use the *plural* (proconsuls) here?

An answer may be found in a report by the Roman historian Tacitus. In *Annals* 13.1, he reports that the proconsul of Ephesus, Silanus, was assassinated and was the first death under Nero. As Keener points out, each proconsul had three deputies, and with the death of the proconsul it would be natural that these three would likely have been filling the late proconsul's position together.[17] We should point out that these events reported by Tacitus appear to correspond well chronologically

---

[14]For more information on Tacitus, see chapter nine.

[15]C. K. Barrett, *Acts of the Apostles: A Shorter Commentary* (New York: T&T Clark, 2002), 301.

[16]Craig S. Keener, *Acts: An Exegetical Commentary: 15:1–23:35* (Grand Rapids, MI: Baker Academic, 2014), 3:2938. Similarly, "Luke is not to be accused of ignorance of an elementary and universally known fact" (Barrett, *Acts of the Apostles*, 301).

[17]Another possibility is that the proconsuls were those who were part of the envoy that assassinated Silanus.

with the events Luke reports in Acts 19, the same time when Paul would have been in Ephesus.

The result, then, is that we have two different texts that are clearly *not* trying to corroborate each other by design. They are, however, illuminating the details and veracity of one another. Luke's use of a plural of proconsuls would have seemed odd to ancient readers who expected only one proconsul. Nevertheless, his use of the plural could, based on Tacitus's report, highlight historically accurate details about a plurality of proconsuls because of the extraordinary events that were unfolding at that time.[18]

CONCLUSION

I have only briefly presented three potential undesigned coincidences. Two of them are internal to the New Testament, and one of them uses a source external to the New Testament. As I noted at the outset, each undesigned coincidence's strength will vary in persuasiveness. Moreover, the force of the overall argument comes in a cumulative case, and these three examples are just a sampling of what such a case would look like. There are several other examples that we could not investigate here but are surely worth considering.[19]

Ultimately, undesigned coincidences add another factor to our case for the reliability of the New Testament. If the New Testament was composed of mass fictions or legends that mutated egregiously over time, then it would be unlikely that we would find these undesigned coincidences between the authors of the New Testament.[20] They thus provide a mark in favor of the New Testament's reliability.

---

[18]We should note that Keener suggests that it is also a "safe guess" to say that Luke is simply using a "generalizing plural" (*Acts* 3:2939). For his whole discussion, see 2937-40. See also Craig S. Keener, *The IVP Bible Background Commentary: New Testament*, 2nd ed. (Downers Grove, IL: InterVarsity Press, 2014), 386-87.

[19]Examples might include why James and John were mending their nets; whether Peter was married; whether Simon of Cyrene is mentioned as the father of Alexander and Rufus; and so on. Many of these can be found in Blunt's *Undesigned Coincidences* or McGrew's *Hidden in Plain View*.

[20]Although the chapter here focused primarily on the Gospels, other works investigate other NT writings and/or OT writings. As the title of Blunt's work suggests, he covers

KEY TAKEAWAYS: UNDESIGNED COINCIDENCES

- Undesigned coincidences are when two texts corroborate each other unintentionally. Additionally, it would be difficult for two sources to support each other if they were both fictional accounts.
- Undesigned coincidences can illuminate two different texts by bringing a bigger picture together, similar to bringing two puzzle pieces together.
- In these instances, the reliability of these reports is increased because of the corroboration between the two accounts. They provide complimentary reports that offer confirmation of each other.

RECOMMENDATIONS

McGrew, Lydia. *Hidden in Plain View: Undesigned Coincidences in the Gospels and Acts*. Chillicothe, OH: DeWard, 2017.

Wallace, J. Warner. *Cold-Case Christianity: A Homicide Detective Investigates the Claims of the Gospels*. Colorado Springs: David Cook, 2013.

Williams, Peter J. *Can We Trust the Gospels?* Wheaton, IL: Crossway, 2018.

both OT and NT writers. McGrew, on the other hand, focuses primarily on the Gospels and Paul's writings.

8

ARCHAEOLOGY

Discoveries of various ancient artifacts or inscriptions can add to the verisimilitude, or credibility, of New Testament reports.[1] Accordingly, archaeology provides another angle from which we can understand the New Testament's reliability. Though many books have been written on the relationship of archaeological discoveries to the Bible, I will briefly present a few examples that have helped add to the authenticity of the New Testament accounts. Like in the previous chapter, here we will consider three examples.

Before we do this, it is important to note that archaeology often adds to the probability of various accounts on a zoomed-out perspective. For example, the discovery of Caiaphas's ossuary provides evidence of his existence, burial, and, given the quality of the ossuary itself, his elite status.[2] This evidence is consistent with what we find in other ancient sources, including the New Testament. However, archaeological evidence is often limited in what it can affirm. This finding, remarkable as it is, does not confirm any discussions Caiaphas had, nor does it confirm any actions he took as high priest. But this finding is consistent with the literary reports that Caiaphas was a member of the elite class and gives an element of truthfulness to those reports. Thus, there are many archaeological discoveries that

---

[1]Verisimilitude has to do with the quality or appearance of being true.

[2]Craig A. Evans, *Jesus and the Remains of His Day: Studies in Jesus and the Evidence of Material Culture* (Peabody, MA: Hendrickson, 2015), 53-54.

tend to add to our wider understanding by increased credibility at the broader (zoomed-out) level.[3]

We also want to be cautious regarding archaeological discoveries because there may have been evidence that was destroyed or lost. Similar to our discussion on New Testament manuscripts, many artifacts have been lost to decay, war, theft, and so on. So we must be careful to avoid the temptation of arguments from silence. In other words, simply because we cannot find archaeological evidence is not, *by itself*, a reason to contend some event, practice, and so on did not occur. Even today, many events do happen, but no physical evidence remains.

A STERN TEMPLE WARNING

In Acts 21:27-36, Paul is accused of having brought a Gentile into the temple area and as a result defiling the temple. The matter is so serious that the crowd quickly attacks Paul. It takes the intervention of Roman soldiers to ultimately stop the crowds from beating Paul. Josephus, a first-century ancient Jewish writer, reports that a warning was posted alongside the temple, and failure to heed the warning could lead to death (Josephus, *Antiquities of the Jews* 15.417; *Jewish War* 6.125-126).[4] Josephus's account corroborates the report of Luke mentioned above. Additionally, it provides a second reference (e.g., multiple attestation) that the Jews were protective of the temple.

In 1871, C. S. Clermont-Ganneau discovered an inscription that contained the very temple warning described by Josephus, and in

---

[3]I am *not* saying that *all* archaeological discoveries are of this zoomed-out nature. One controversial piece of evidence that could be an example of a zoomed-in piece of information is the shroud of Turin, which is considered by some to be the burial cloth of Jesus. Although recent scholarship by Tristan Casabianca and others has offered serious challenges to the view that the shroud was made in the Middle Ages, this artifact—one of the most studied in history—is beyond our scope here. See Casabianca et al., "Radiocarbon Dating of the Turin Shroud: New Evidence from Raw Data," *Archaeometry* 61, no. 5 (2019): 1223-31. On the shroud in general, see, at the popular level, Mary and Alan Whanger, *The Shroud of Turin: An Adventure in Discovery* (Franklin, TN: Providence House, 1998). For a more technical work, see Mark Antonacci, *Test the Shroud at the Atomic and Molecular Levels* (Brentwood, TN: Forefront, 2016).

[4]Noting also that the sign appeared in Greek and Latin (*Jewish War* 5.194).

1935 a second inscription was found with similar but fragmentary wording. The inscription is in Greek and says the following: "NO FOREIGNER MAY ENTER WITHIN THE BARRICADE WHICH SURROUNDS THE TEMPLE AND ENCLOSURE. ANYONE WHO IS CAUGHT DOING SO WILL HAVE HIMSELF TO THANK FOR HIS ENSUING DEATH."[5] This archaeological find provides insight into the texts of Paul and Josephus. The reports associated with the temple warning are shown to have authenticity with respect to this archaeological find.

Paul was likely well aware of this warning before the incident reported in Acts 21. Despite what his accusers thought, Paul had no desire to defile the temple. After all, Paul was not found to have defiled pagan temples; how much more unlikely would it have been for him to defile the temple of the true God?[6] As Acts indicates, Paul defiled neither.

This inscription might also shed light on Paul's comment in Ephesians 2:14, when he writes, "For He Himself is our peace, who made both groups into one and broke down the barrier of the dividing wall." Some have understood Paul's comments here to be a metaphor of the temple barrier, which separated Gentiles and Jews.[7] The wall that separated the two groups at the temple was removed in the work and person of Jesus as he brought reconciliation to the world (see Gal 3:28). This barrier is now gone, and there is no longer a dividing wall between the two groups.

This inscription helps clarify what we find in the New Testament (as well as Josephus). It adds concrete evidence that there were severe repercussions for those who violated the warning. It was a life-and-death

---

[5]F. F. Bruce, *The New Testament Documents: Are They Reliable?*, 6th ed. (Grand Rapids, MI: Eerdmans, 1981), 95. A similar translation is found in Peretz Segal, "The Penalty of the Warning Inscription from the Temple of Jerusalem," *Israel Exploration Journal* 39, no. 1/2 (1989): 79.

[6]Craig S. Keener, *Acts: An Exegetical Commentary: 15:1–23:35* (Grand Rapids, MI: Baker Academic, 2014), 3:3146. For his full discussion for this episode, see 3144-54.

[7]Bruce, *New Testament Documents*, 95. More recently, Darrell Bock considers this as one of three possibilities. See Bock, *Ephesians: An Introduction and Commentary*, Tyndale New Testament Commentaries 10 (Downers Grove, IL: InterVarsity Press, 2019), 77-79.

matter. Moreover, the warning was perhaps appropriated by Paul and used as a metaphor.

CRUCIFIXION VICTIM: YEHOHANAN

Just over fifty years ago, in 1968, an incredible discovery helped shed light on questions related to ancient crucifixion and burial practices. This discovery occurred at a burial site in Jerusalem where thirty-five bodies were found. These bodies were located within fifteen separate ossuaries. (An ossuary is a box into which an ancient Jewish person or persons would have had their bones placed about a year after death. Typically, a body would initially be placed in a burial location, such as one of the several rock-cut chambers found in Jerusalem, and about a year later the bones would be collected and placed into an ossuary.)

In one of the ossuaries a Jewish man was found who had evidently been crucified before being properly buried. His name, etched on the side of the ossuary, was Yehohanan. Significantly, the contents of this ossuary "date to the late 20s CE, that is, during the administration of Pilate, the very prefect who condemned Jesus to the cross."[8] The remains clearly show that a nail had gone through the victim's heel bone.

This nail turned out to be very significant. It was not straight like a normal nail but rather had a hook at the end of it, sort of like a fishing hook. The bend at the end of the nail was *created after* the nail went into the victim and the wood beam. So as the straight nail went into the bone, it then struck something in the wood, causing it to bend so that it would not come out. Some think that this occurred because the nail hit a knot in the wood as it was driven into the cross. As a result, the executioners were unable to remove the nail and thus took the entire section off so that the body could properly be buried.[9]

---

[8]Evans, *Jesus and the Remains*, 121. Similarly, "Jehohanan was crucified closer to the time of Jesus' own crucifixion." Joseph Zias and James H. Charlesworth, "Crucifixion: Archeology, Jesus, and the Dead Sea Scrolls," in *Jesus and the Dead Sea Scrolls* (New York: Doubleday, 1995), 284.

[9]Nails could be used multiple times, so soldiers would attempt to take them out and reuse them when possible.

This finding is significant for at least two reasons.[10] First, here is archaeological evidence corroborating that nails were used in crucifixion practices. In ancient literature, reports that attest to the use of nails during crucifixion are plentiful.[11] This finding provides an additional layer of confirmation to these reports.

Second, and more importantly, this finding is significant because it validates what other literary texts indicate—namely, crucifixion victims could receive a proper burial and would ultimately be placed into an ossuary.[12] Jews during this period were very concerned with burial practices. This followed from Deuteronomy 21:22-23, which states, "If a person has committed a sin carrying a sentence of death and he is put to death, and you hang him on a tree, his body is not to be left overnight on the tree, but you shall certainly bury him on the same day (for he who is hanged is cursed of God), so that you do not defile your land which the LORD your God is giving you as an inheritance." Accordingly, an important and biblical concern was to bury the dead, even the crucified, to keep the land undefiled.

Such victims would *not* have been thrown into a pit or mass grave, where their bodies could not be distinguished from one another, as has occasionally been suggested. Princeton professor James Charlesworth concludes that the "old hypothesis that Jesus' corpse *must* have been dumped into a pit set aside for the corpses of criminals and insurrectionists and not buried is disproved. Jehohanan's bones had received a proper Jewish burial."[13] Similarly, Jewish scholar Shimon Gibson states that this finding contradicts "the notion that crucified criminals were

[10]James Charlesworth believes this to be one of the top archaeological findings related to Jesus. See James H. Charlesworth, *Jesus Within Judaism: New Light from Exciting Archaeological Discoveries* (New York: Doubleday, 1988), 122.

[11]For a list of original sources, see Martin Hengel, *Crucifixion: In the Ancient World and the Folly of the Message of the Cross* (Philadelphia: Fortress, 1977), 31-32 (and related footnotes). Hengel's work is a concise yet robust historical assessment of crucifixion practices.

[12]For nuances to this, see Craig A. Evans, "Getting the Burial Traditions and Evidence Right," in *How God Became Jesus: The Real Origins of Belief in Jesus' Divine Nature—A Response to Bart D. Ehrman*, ed. Michael F. Bird (Grand Rapids, MI: Zondervan, 2014), 71-93.

[13]Charlesworth, *Jesus Within Judaism*, 123.

subsequently buried disgracefully like dogs and without the dignity of a final repose."[14]

Additionally, Jewish communities during this time were familiar with placing a body in a rock-cut tomb in such a way that it was identifiable a year later. The bones of that body could then be properly placed into an ossuary. Yehohanan provides archaeological evidence of just such practices. Craig Evans concludes that the "reburial of the bones of Yehohanan . . . demonstrates that the Jewish people knew how to note and remember the place of primary burial."[15] This finding adds that *crucifixion victims* were also included in the group of Jews who were able to, *and did*, receive a proper burial.

FIVE PORTICOES

John 5:2 states, "In Jerusalem, by the Sheep Gate, there is a pool which in Hebrew is called Bethesda, having five porticoes." This description was often dismissed as a fictional creation of John designed to function as a theological truth. Perhaps the five porticoes reflected the Pentateuch, and John's meaning referred to something other than an actual location. Indeed, Charlesworth notes that this text of John was "dismissed as allegorical theology."[16] Part of the reason for this is that there were no other ancient descriptions of such a pool, nor were there any archaeological findings of a pool with five porticoes.

However, this all changed once the pool with five porticoes was discovered.[17] Within the Sheep Gate were found two pools with four porticoes around and one separating the two pools. Shimon Gibson, who personally worked on the site, explains that it was used "specifically for ritual purity" and that it could not have been used to collect

[14]Shimon Gibson, *The Final Days of Jesus: The Archaeological Evidence* (New York: HarperOne, 2009), 132; see also 110-15.

[15]Craig A. Evans, *Jesus and His World: The Archaeological Evidence* (Louisville, KY: Westminster John Knox, 2012), 137.

[16]Charlesworth, *Jesus Within Judaism*, 120.

[17]Charlesworth considers this to be within the top five archaeological discoveries for the historical Jesus (*Jesus Within Judaism*, 119). In addition to this finding, literary manuscripts were also discovered in Qumran that appear to make mention of the pool.

drinking water or as a pool for mere entertainment.[18] Interestingly, Gibson also points out that "the landings at different intervals would evidently have been used for the placing of the beds of disabled people, as John implies (5:3)."[19] Those with physical disabilities would have been unable to use normal steps, and if John's depiction is accurate, then we would expect to find exactly the types of landings mentioned by Gibson. Thus, not only does the discovery of the pools and porticoes confirm that John was making historically accurate remarks regarding this location, but the fact that those with disabilities could use this pool also gives further credibility to John's account.

OTHER FINDINGS

There are several other significant archaeological discoveries that I can mention only in brief here. One of them is the Delphi inscription, which provides information about when Gallio was proconsul of Corinth. The inscription says the following: "Tiberius [Claudius] Caesar Augustus Germanicus . . . [in his tribunician] power [year 12, acclaimed emperor] the twenty-sixth time, father of the country. . . . [Lucius] Junius Gallio my friend and [pro]consul [of Achaia wrote] . . ." As Everett Ferguson concludes, "Gallio's governorship must have occurred between the summer of 51 and the summer of 52."[20] We know this because a proconsul served only a one-year term.

As we saw in chapter three, Paul stayed in Corinth a "year and six months," according to Acts 18:11. Significantly, Paul's stay in Corinth coincided with Gallio's time as proconsul. In fact, Acts 18:12-17 says that groups were unhappy with Paul and sought help from Gallio directly. This finding is vital in helping to develop an accurate chronology for Paul's missionary activity and writings.

Other significant findings might include archaeological evidence related to Pontius Pilate. Some of the coins minted during his reign

---

[18]Gibson, *Final Days of Jesus*, 75.

[19]Gibson, *Final Days of Jesus*, 76.

[20]Everett Ferguson, *Backgrounds of Early Christianity*, 3rd ed. (Grand Rapids, MI: Eerdmans, 2003), 585.

shed light on how he ruled (whether seeking to be a provocateur or not), while a stone in Caesarea Maritima has his name and position inscribed.[21] I noted in the introduction above that Caiaphas's ossuary was discovered and is important given his status as high priest during Jesus' trial (e.g., Mt 26:3, 57).

Another archaeological discovery is an inscription found on a marble slab in Nazareth that warns against grave robbing or tampering with the seal of a tomb and is dated to the first century. Last, the Palatine graffito is a picture of a crucifixion victim with a donkey's head. Below the image are inscribed the words, "Alexamenos worships (his) God," which is likely a mocking reference to Jesus. The list could go on, with several findings of varying significance for the New Testament.[22]

CONCLUSION

In this chapter I sought to highlight some archaeological findings and how they add another level of reliability to the New Testament. Indeed, William Ramsay provides a helpful illustration of this reality. Though Ramsay approached the archaeological data from a skeptical position, he was ultimately compelled to change his mind as he observed the archaeological evidence.[23] Here I have been able to provide only a small introductory sample of the archaeological evidence, but even in this brief discussion, we have seen how archaeological findings corroborate details in the New Testament. Accordingly, archaeological findings provide another reason for considering the New Testament reliable.

---

[21]Evans, *Jesus and the Remains*, 58-59. Evans helpfully points out that Pilate is referred to as a "prefect" and that Tacitus's reference to Pilate as a "procurator" is anachronistic.

[22]Charlesworth presents a list of the archaeological findings he believes to be the most significant to studying the historical Jesus (*Jesus Within Judaism*, 104-27).

[23]Ramsay's story is summarized in Edwin M. Yamauchi, *The Stones and the Scriptures* (Philadelphia: J. B. Lippincott/A Holman Book, 1972), 92-125. Within these pages Yamauchi highlights the findings of William Ramsay and how they challenged the skeptical interpretations of the Tübingen school. Although Ramsay initially held to a more unreliable portrait that was close to the Tübingen theory, the evidence ultimately caused him to change his mind. Yamauchi's chapter is aptly titled "Ramsay vs. the Tübingen School." For a briefer account see Bruce, *New Testament Documents*, 91-93.

KEY TAKEAWAYS: ARCHAEOLOGY

- Archaeology is a somewhat distinctive category for studying the past. It can confirm physical remains but typically adds verisimilitude to reported events (e.g., Caiaphas's tomb compared with the words and actions of Caiaphas).
- There are several archaeological finds that contribute to our knowledge of the New Testament and add to its reliability.
- Among these important findings are the temple warning and Yehohanan the crucifixion victim.

RECOMMENDED READING

Charlesworth, James H. *Jesus and Archaeology*. Grand Rapids, MI: Eerdmans, 2006.

Evans, Craig A. *Jesus and the Remains of His Day: Studies in Jesus and the Evidence of Material Culture*. Peabody, MA: Hendrickson, 2015.

Price, J. Randall, and H. Wayne House. *Zondervan Handbook of Biblical Archaeology: A Book by Book Guide to Archaeological Discoveries Related to the Bible*. Grand Rapids, MI: Zondervan, 2017.

9

NON-CHRISTIAN SOURCES

Non-Christian sources are one of the more popular avenues used to demonstrate the reliability of the New Testament. I mentioned some ways in which this might occur in chapters six and seven, but here I will focus on critical sources that overlap with New Testament reports. These sources add to our understanding of the New Testament, reflecting a zoomed-in view on a map regarding specific events or beliefs.

NON-CHRISTIAN SOURCES IN CONTEXT

Two points need to be briefly mentioned before introducing non-Christian sources. The first has to do with why non-Christian sources would be interested in Jesus and/or Christians, and the second has to do with the reliability of the New Testament itself. These two considerations will help us better understand the relationship between these sources.

First, we should remember that Christianity began as a minority movement within the Greco-Roman world and presented a *vastly different* worldview from those around it.[1] For the wider culture, power, dominance, and control were the virtues of the day in many ways. Oppression was a commonsense view and not considered a bad thing in the ancient world but rather a demonstration of one's power and ability over others. The greater power one had, the greater influence in the world one would have.

[1]For a helpful description of this from an agnostic, see Tom Holland, *Dominion: How the Christian Revolution Remade the World* (New York: Basic Books, 2019).

Since such a worldview dominated the broader culture, we must wonder why those who sought glory in power and control would be concerned with someone who, like so many unnamed others, died in Roman Palestine, on a cross no less. Indeed, Paul was all too aware that the gospel message challenged this mindset. He notes, for example, that "we preach Christ crucified, to Jews a stumbling block, and to Gentiles foolishness" (1 Cor 1:23). The very message of the gospel centered on an individual who was defeated by enemies and died a shameful death.[2]

Consequently, we might expect non-Christian references to Jesus within the first one hundred or so years of his life to be rather rare. Robert Van Voorst, in his work on extrabiblical sources, concludes that "Christ was not nearly such an important issue for Rome, to judge from surviving Roman writings. The empire and its government were occupied with other matters that seemed much more serious to them, as the proportion of treatment Tacitus, Suetonius, and Pliny gave to Christ suggests."[3] Romans were not typically interested in the origins of minority religious leaders or groups (such as the Druids or Jews), nor were they generally concerned with the founders of messianic movements. However, as we will see below, rather than Jesus himself, discussion on "Christianity as a movement is their primary, perhaps their only, concern."[4] Accordingly, one reason we might see Jesus or Christianity mentioned by non-Christian authors is the interaction of Christians with the wider Roman world.

The second point to emphasize is one I have been making throughout the book—namely, the reliability of the New Testament writings on their own grounds. I want to emphasize that just because an author is a Christian, this does not *automatically* negate what that author reports.[5] It merely bids us to be aware of the author's bias (as well as our own).[6]

---

[2]Recall in our discussion on archaeology the image of Alexamenos.

[3]Robert E. Van Voorst, *Jesus Outside the New Testament: An Introduction to the Ancient Evidence* (Grand Rapids, MI: Eerdmans, 2000), 69. Voorst provides a series of other helpful considerations in his conclusion that are also worth exploring (68-74).

[4]Van Voorst, *Jesus Outside the New Testament*, 72.

[5]For an introduction to some ways in which historians can ascertain reliable data, see James H. Charlesworth, *The Historical Jesus: An Essential Guide* (Nashville: Abingdon, 2008), 15-32.

[6]See the excellent discussion in N. T. Wright, *The New Testament and the People of God*, Christian Origins and the Question of God 1 (Minneapolis: Fortress, 1992), 89.

Too often, an unnecessary emphasis is placed on non-Christian sources as though they were somehow neutral sources and free from bias. As I have been highlighting, the New Testament sources are historically good sources in their own right. In the case of the Gospels, they predate the non-Christian sources by decades and were written by those far closer to the events themselves.

It is ironic that a non-Christian may help to further illustrate this point. Skeptic Bart Ehrman argues that no historian would reject early accounts from the Revolutionary War just because their authors were Americans. They should be used as significant sources. This includes accounts from George Washington and his supporters. "To refuse to use them as sources," Ehrman writes, "is to sacrifice the most important avenues to the past we have, and on purely ideological, not historical, grounds." What is the implication for the Gospels? "So too the Gospels."[7]

Ultimately, we want to be careful to avoid excessive, unnecessarily, and arbitrarily limiting demands. The above comments should also help give some perspective regarding the value of these sources. To be clear, I am not saying that the sources are of no value, for they certainly contribute to our understanding of the New Testament and beyond. Nevertheless, I want to identify their proper position with respect to New Testament claims.

NOTABLE NON-CHRISTIAN SOURCES

We can now turn to some comments from non-Christian sources regarding Jesus. While there are several different sources, I will limit us to three prominent examples. Here I will discuss Josephus, Tacitus, and Pliny the Younger.[8]

---

[7]Bart D. Ehrman, *Did Jesus Exist? The Historical Argument for Jesus of Nazareth* (New York: HarperOne, 2012), 74. One should note that agnostic Maurice Casey focuses on NT texts in his discussions with the most extreme skeptics. See Casey, *Jesus: Evidence and Argument or Mythicist Myths?* (London: Bloomsbury T&T Clark, 2014).

[8]These are not the only non-Christian authors who refer to Jesus or Christianity. Others typically found in these discussions include Suetonius, Mara bar Serapion, and Thallus, among others.

Josephus:* Antiquities of the Jews *18.3 and 20.9. Josephus (ca. AD 37–97) was a prominent Jew who also became a prominent Roman after a failed Jewish rebellion. He wrote several works before the close of the first century. So, he was writing reasonably close to the events he described and was in a good position to know various aspects of Judaism during this period.

There are two relevant texts for our discussions here, and they both come from his work *Antiquities of the Jews*. The first is a reference to Jesus in *Antiquities* 18.3. The second mentions James, Jesus' brother, in *Antiquities* 20.9.

For various reasons, scholars think that the first text of Josephus was likely tampered with by later Christian scribes to some degree. It is helpful to summarize briefly why this is the case. Early Christian writers state that Josephus was *not* a Christian, but Josephus's text, as it appears now, gives a very optimistic description of Jesus. This has led scholars to debate whether Josephus's text as we have it now was tampered with and, if so, how much? If it was tampered with, can we reconstruct an original? Scholars *do* think the text was tampered with, but to a minimal extent. They also think a reasonable reconstruction of Josephus's text can be made, with some caution, and the apparent Christian gloss removed.[9]

For our purposes here, we simply want to be aware of the concern, and additional technical issues need not detain us further.[10] I present the more "neutral" text that many scholars accept. Following John Meier's reconstruction, Josephus says the following:

> At this time there appeared Jesus, a wise man. For he was a doer of startling deeds, a teacher of people who receive the truth with pleasure. And he gained a following both among many Jews and among many of Greek origin. And when Pilate, because of an

---

[9]Assistance in this re-creation is also provided by an Arabic source of Josephus's text. See comments below.

[10]For those interested, see any number of discussions on the subject in John P. Meier, *A Marginal Jew: Rethinking the Historical Jesus*, vol. 1, *The Roots and the Problem of the Person*, Anchor Bible Reference Library (New York: Doubleday, 1991), 56-88; Gary R. Habermas, *The Historical Jesus: Ancient Evidence for the Life of Christ* (Joplin, MO: College Press, 1996), 192-96; Van Voorst, *Jesus Outside the New Testament*, 81-104.

> accusation made by the leading men among us, condemned him to the cross, those who had loved him previously did not cease to do so. And up until this very day the tribe of Christians (named after him) has not died out.[11]

Several facts are highlighted from this text that corroborate what is found in the New Testament. Jesus was considered to have been wise and did things that amazed people. There were many people who followed Jesus. Ultimately, Jesus was condemned to be crucified under Pilate at the instigation of Jewish leaders. Those who followed him were called Christians, and they did not abandon Jesus after the brutality and embarrassment of the crucifixion but rather were still around in Josephus's time.

The second reference in Josephus is considerably briefer. Here Josephus mentions Jesus and his brother James. He writes, "Festus was now dead, and Albinus was but upon the road; so he assembled the Sanhedrim of judges, and brought before them the brother of Jesus, who was called Christ, whose name was James, and some others and when he had formed an accusation against them as breakers of the law, he delivered them to be stoned."[12] Many recognize that Jesus receives only a passing comment here because Josephus discussed Jesus earlier, in 18.3. This text not only discusses the martyrdom of James but also highlights that Jesus had a brother named James and that Jesus was also called Christ (or Messiah). Both of these claims are found in the New Testament (e.g., Gal 1:19).

JOSEPHUS'S CORROBORATION

1. Jesus was considered wise and did various deeds that garnered attention.
2. Jesus had many followers.

[11]Meier, *Marginal Jew* 1:61; similarly Van Voorst, *Jesus Outside the New Testament*, 93. It is worth noting that an Arabic version was found that includes a clause that mentions Jesus appearing to his followers after the crucifixion. See Shlomo Pines, *An Arabic Version of the Testimonium Flavianum and Its Implications* (Jerusalem: Israel Academy of Sciences and Humanities, 1971), 16; see also Habermas, *Historical Jesus*, 193-94; Van Voorst, *Jesus Outside the New Testament*, 97-98.

[12]Josephus, *Antiquities* 20.9, in *The Works of Flavius Josephus*, trans. William Whiston (London, 1737).

3. Jesus was condemned to crucifixion under Pilate due to the accusation of Jewish leaders.
4. His followers continued to love and follow him even after his death.
5. Christians were still around in Josephus's day.
6. Jesus was referred to as the Christ.
7. Jesus had a brother named James, who was about to be stoned.

Tacitus:* Annals *15.44. Cornelius Tacitus (ca. AD 55–120) was a member of the Roman aristocracy and provides an immense amount of historical information regarding ancient Rome. Of his writings, the two best-known are *Annals* and *Histories*. He relates information regarding Christianity insofar as it was connected to a major fire that occurred in Rome around AD 64, during the reign of Nero.

Tacitus reports that there were suspicions that Nero was responsible for starting the fire and that, to avoid blame, Nero blamed the Christians and punished them severely as a result. Tacitus writes,

> Consequently, to get rid of the report, Nero fastened the guilt and inflicted the most exquisite tortures on a class hated for their abominations, called Christians by the populace. Christus, from whom the name had its origin, suffered the extreme penalty during the reign of Tiberius at the hands of one of our procurators, Pontius Pilatus, and a most mischievous superstition, thus checked for the moment, again broke out not only in Judaea, the first source of the evil, but even in Rome.[13]

It is worth noting that in the same passage, Tacitus also reports that "even for criminals who deserved extreme and exemplary punishment, there arose a feeling of compassion; for it was not, as it seemed, for the public good, but to glut one man's cruelty, that they were being

[13]Tacitus, *Annals* 15.44. Hadas, Moses, ed. *The Complete Works of Tacitus. Translated by Alfred John Church and William Jackson Brodribb* (New York: Modern Library, 1942).

destroyed" (*Annals* 15.44). Nero was so cruel to these Christians that it began to evoke compassion toward them.

Tacitus includes much information that intersects with the New Testament. For example, Christians were named by the populace after their founder ("Christus"), who suffered the "extreme penalty" (crucifixion) under Pilate. Tacitus says the movement appears to have originated in Judea and was briefly checked but broke out again and made its way to Rome.

TACITUS'S CORROBORATION

1. Christians were disdained by the public and horrifically persecuted by Nero.
2. Jesus was executed during the reign of Pontius Pilate. He suffered the "extreme penalty" (crucifixion).
3. The Jesus movement stopped "for the moment" after Jesus' death but then grew considerably, starting in Judea.
4. Christians eventually made their way to Rome.

***Pliny the Younger:* Book *10*, Letter *96 (and 97)*.** Pliny the Younger (ca. AD 61–113) held a number of different positions within the Roman government. He was so well connected within the Roman government that his comments about Christians are found in a letter written to the emperor Trajan (around AD 112). His letter and Trajan's response are both well worth reading in their entirety.

Pliny wrote to Trajan because he had procedural questions on how to treat Christians that were being interrogated (and in some cases tortured or killed). He sought Trajan's advice on handling such cases since he had not been involved in them before. Pliny was unaware of the normal punishments for Christians and unclear about whether they should be punished just for being Christian even if they were not guilty of other crimes, how far investigations should be pursued, and so forth. Additionally, he was concerned about anonymous pamphlets that were circulating and accused certain people of being Christian.

Pliny says that his current practice was to try to get the accused Christian to recant. He would ask the person multiple times whether they were a Christian and warn them that if they continued to say yes, then they would be executed.[14] Those who denied they were Christian, Pliny would dismiss after "they had repeated after me a formula of invocation to the gods and had made offerings of wine and incense to your statue (which I had ordered to be brought into court for this purpose along with the images of the gods), and furthermore had reviled the name of Christ: none of which things, I understand, any genuine Christian can be induced to do."[15] Interestingly, those who recanted provided Pliny with information about Christianity. They do not appear to have been guilty of any crimes (see 1 Pet 3:16-17) but rather

> the sum total of their guilt or error amounted to no more than this: they had met regularly before dawn on a fixed day to chant verses alternately among themselves in honour of Christ as if to a god, and also to bind themselves by oath, not for any criminal purpose, but to abstain from theft, robbery and adultery, to commit no breach of trust and not to deny a deposit when called upon to restore it. After this ceremony it had been their custom to disperse and reassemble later to take food of an ordinary, harmless kind.[16]

This comment is important since, as Van Voorst highlights, it is the "first non-Christian description of early Christian worship."[17] Moreover, we can see that Christians not only worshiped Jesus but committed themselves to honesty while turning away from immorality (see Eph 4:17–5:21).

---

[14]Pliny thought such stubbornness to recant was an offense in itself.

[15]Pliny the Younger, *Book* 10, *Letter* 96, in *Letters*, vol. 2, *Books 8-10. Panegyricus*, trans. Betty Radice, Loeb Classical Library 59 (Cambridge, MA: Harvard University Press, 1969). "Genuine Christians" would not deny Christ or worship another; however, recall Peter's three denials. Those who denied being Christian in the face of persecutions raised various challenges for the early church since some who recanted being a Christian also regretted their denial.

[16]Pliny the Younger, *Book* 10, *Letter* 96, trans. Radice.

[17]Van Voorst, *Jesus Outside the New Testament*, 27.

Pliny then goes on to note that another reason for his consulting Trajan was that a "great many individuals" were being brought for trials, coming from all ages, genders, and classes. This led to the temples being "almost entirely deserted" as well. Pliny was thus hoping Trajan could properly direct him on how to conduct these trials since he did not believe they would be ceasing any time soon.

Trajan's response to Pliny's inquiry is relatively brief, and I will present it in its entirety here:

> You have followed the right course of procedure, my dear Pliny, in your examination of the cases of persons charged with being Christians, for it is impossible to lay down a general rule to a fixed formula. These people must not be hunted out; if they are brought before you and the charge against them is proved, they must be punished, but in the case of anyone who denies that he is a Christian, and makes it clear that he is not by offering prayers to our gods, he is to be pardoned as a result of his repentance however suspect his past conduct may be. But pamphlets circulated anonymously must play no part in any accusation. They create the worst sort of precedent and are quite out of keeping with the spirit of our age.[18]

Pliny is thus urged to continue trying to get Christians to recant but to refrain from proactively seeking out Christians. Moreover, Trajan says anonymous accusations should have no part in these trials.

CONCLUSION

These sources may seem like trivial items that corroborate basic New Testament teachings; however, their significance should not be overlooked. Consider, for example, what if, instead of saying that Jesus' death occurred in Judea, Tacitus reported that Jesus died in Greece? Or, perhaps, rather than Jesus' being condemned as a criminal, what if Josephus reported that Jesus died during a battle in Galilee? Differences

---

[18]Pliny the Younger, *Book* 10, *Letter* 97, trans. Radice.

like these would certainly and understandably raise a number of questions.[19] Fortunately, this is not the case. Rather, non-Christian sources frequently corroborate New Testament claims. Thus, these reports add more weight to the reliability of the New Testament.

KEY TAKEAWAYS: NON-CHRISTIAN SOURCES

- There are multiple non-Christian sources outside the New Testament that reference either Jesus or early Christians.
- Despite apparently being tampered with, Josephus's text can reasonably be reconstructed and provides an important non-Christian source for Jesus. Tacitus and Pliny the Younger also provide important comments about Jesus and early Christianity.
- These sources corroborate the information we have in the New Testament. They do not, for example, claim that Jesus was crucified in Egypt or Greece.

RECOMMENDED READING

Bruce, F. F. *Jesus and Christian Origins Outside the New Testament*. London: Hodder & Stoughton, 1974.

Habermas, Gary R. *The Historical Jesus: Ancient Evidence for the Life of Christ*. Joplin, MO: College Press, 1996.

Van Voorst, Robert E. *Jesus Outside the New Testament: An Introduction to the Ancient Evidence*. Grand Rapids, MI: Eerdmans, 2000.

[19]Noting the corroboration of Jesus' existence as opposed to a mythical figure of the past. See Van Voorst, *Jesus Outside the New Testament*, 73. The biggest discrepancies one finds in this regard are in later Jewish sources (Babylonian Talmud Sanhedrin 43a), though these sources have numerous issues that cannot be discussed here.

10

NONCANONICAL CHRISTIAN SOURCES

While the last chapter presented non-Christian sources, this chapter will present noncanonical Christian sources. In other words, these are early Christian sources *outside* the New Testament. I pointed out in chapter nine that historians do not simply discount a source just because it is Christian.[1] The same holds true in this chapter as well. Indeed, the Christian sources in this chapter are regarded, even by skeptics, as important independent sources of information.[2]

These authors will help provide both zoomed-out and zoomed-in perspectives of New Testament reliability. For example, Clement notes the martyrdom of Peter and Paul, which provides a zoomed-out consideration regarding their teachings because it is strong evidence that they genuinely believed what they taught. Note that a specific event or teaching is not in view here, but their willingness to suffer and die certainly colors our understanding of their teachings in general and central teachings in particular (e.g., Jesus'

---

[1]Recall that historians would not exclude American sources when examining the Revolutionary War. One might add that neither would historians ignore Jewish sources when studying the Holocaust. Other similar examples abound.

[2]Bart D. Ehrman, *Did Jesus Exist? The Historical Argument for Jesus of Nazareth* (New York: HarperOne, 2012), 98-105. Ehrman covers Papias, Ignatius, and Clement. Concerning Papias, he states, "This is not eyewitness testimony to the life of Jesus, but it is getting very close to that. . . . This then is testimony that is independent of the Gospels themselves" (101).

resurrection).[3] On the other end, we find a more zoomed-in perspective when Clement mentions the discord of the Corinthian church that Paul was addressing in 1 Corinthians 1:12. Clement offers early confirmation of both Paul's first letter to the Corinthian church and the factionalism that Paul was trying to correct.

I should note that this chapter will not contain Gnostic writings, as they are later and beyond the scope of the present work.[4] However, I will cover some of these works in the next chapter since they are related to discussions on the development of the New Testament canon. Moreover, the sources covered here are those that the early church thought were valuable but not on the same level as Scripture. The focus of this chapter, then, will be on some of the earliest Christian works outside the New Testament. These will be the writings of Clement of Rome, Ignatius of Antioch, and Polycarp of Smyrna.

CLEMENT OF ROME

We have a letter to the church in Corinth that was written before the end of the first century (ca. AD 65–95). This letter is attributed to Clement (often considered the same Clement of Phil 4:3), though the letter states it is from the church in Rome. Early church writers indicate that Clement was a bishop of the church of Rome.

Like Paul's letters to the Corinthian church, Clement's letter was written to deal with ongoing factionalism within the church at Corinth. Clement reveals several details that illuminate our understanding of the New Testament. As noted above, Clement's letter informs us of the martyrdoms of both Peter and Paul. Clement writes:

---

[3]An example of how this applies to a specific event should be noted. Peter and Paul are reported to have seen the risen Jesus personally. It is unlikely that they knowingly lied about their own personal and direct experiences and were then willing to suffer and die as a result. This adds significant weight to their testimony and is different from others who died for their beliefs.

[4]Gnosticism developed primarily in the second through fourth centuries and was considered heretical by the early church. In the late second century, Irenaeus discusses many Gnostic teachings in *Against Heresies*, as he had traveled to Rome to study many of them firsthand.

> Let us set before our eyes the illustrious apostles. Peter, through unrighteous envy, endured not one or two, but numerous labours; and when he had at length suffered martyrdom, departed to the place of glory due to him. Owing to envy, Paul also obtained the reward of patient endurance, after being seven times thrown into captivity, compelled to flee, and stoned. After preaching both in the east and west, he gained the illustrious reputation due to his faith, having taught righteousness to the whole world, and come to the extreme limit of the west, and suffered martyrdom under the prefects. Thus was he removed from the world and went into the holy place, having proved himself a striking example of patience. (1 Clement 5)[5]

The sufferings and martyrdoms of Peter and Paul are important as they highlight the genuine beliefs these men held regarding their experiences (see 1 Cor 15:32). We thus have good reasons to believe that Peter and Paul were not lying but rather telling the truth about things they directly experienced firsthand and knew to be true. Another important aspect to note is that Clement (and the Christians in Rome) saw both Peter and Paul as models worth following. Though some have attempted to suggest a rift between Peter and Paul, this text presents both as unified in their message and examples for Christians to follow (see 1 Cor 15:11; Gal 1:18–2:10).

Atheist/agnostic New Testament scholar Bart Ehrman points out that Clement's letter provides an "independent witness not just to the life of Jesus as a historical figure but to some of his teachings and deeds."[6] An example is in 1 Clement 13, which summarizes aspects of the Sermon on the Mount (Mt 6:12-15; 7:2; Lk 6:36-38). Here Clement wants the church in Corinth to "be mindful of the words of the Lord Jesus."

This letter also corroborates the problems of factionalism within the Corinthian church that Paul mentioned. I noted above that this is a

[5]All citations in this chapter follow the translation of Alexander Roberts and James Donaldson, eds., *The Ante-Nicene Fathers*, vol. 1 (Peabody, MA: Hendrickson, 1995).

[6]Ehrman, *Did Jesus Exist?*, 105. Ehrman includes a list of eleven bullet points regarding the historical Jesus that are found in 1 Clement.

zoomed-in piece of corroboration, since it addresses specific events, and here Clement encourages the Corinthians to "take up the epistle of the blessed Apostle Paul. What did he write to you at the time when the Gospel first began to be preached? Truly, under the inspiration of the Spirit, he wrote to you concerning himself, and Cephas, and Apollos, because even then parties had been formed among you" (1 Clement 47). Here there is a clear connection to 1 Corinthians 1:12, where he discourages the Corinthians from such divisions. Clement's concerns are that the Corinthians have not learned their lessons and the situation is worse now than before.

IGNATIUS OF ANTIOCH

Ignatius of was the bishop of Antioch and martyred in Rome around AD 110. While being taken to Rome and under guard, he wrote at least seven letters. Ignatius's letters were written to several churches, including the church in Rome, in which he encourages believers to refrain from intervening in his execution.[7] He also wrote a letter to Polycarp, the bishop of Smyrna, whom I will briefly discuss below. In these letters we find various areas of overlap with New Testament reports.

According to Ehrman, Ignatius provides "another independent witness to the life of Jesus. . . . He cannot be shown to have been relying on the Gospels. And he was bishop in Antioch, the city where both Peter and Paul spent considerable time in the preceding generation. . . . His views too can trace a lineage straight back to apostolic times."[8] For example, three letters include mentions or reminders of Jesus' death as

---

[7]The other churches Ignatius wrote to were those in Ephesus, Magnesia, Tralles, Philadelphia, and Smyrna. Johannes Quasten considers the "most important" letter to be the one written to Rome. See Quasten, *Patrology: The Beginnings of Patristic Literature* (Allen, TX: Christian Classics, 1983), 1:64. Undoubtedly part of the reason for this is the moving comments Ignatius makes in requesting the church at Rome to *not* hinder his pending martyrdom, with comments such as, "I am the wheat of God, and let me be ground by the teeth of wild beasts, that I may be found the pure bread of Christ. Rather entice the wild beasts, that they may become my tomb" (Ignatius, *To the Romans* 4).

[8]Ehrman, *Did Jesus Exist?*, 103-4. One should note that Ehrman does *not* think Ignatius is too late of a source to provide valuable information regarding Jesus (or early Christianity) even though this letter was written around AD 110.

having occurred during the reign of Pontius Pilate. In his letter to the church at Magnesia, he encourages believers to "attain to full assurance in regard to the birth, and passion, and resurrection which took place in the time of the government of Pontius Pilate, being truly and certainly accomplished by Jesus Christ, who is our hope, from which may no one of you ever be turned aside" (Ignatius, *To the Magnesians* 11).

Similar comments are found in his letter to the church in Tralles, where he writes that Jesus "was truly persecuted under Pontius Pilate; He was truly crucified, and [truly] died, in the sight of beings in heaven, and on earth, and under the earth. He was also truly raided from the dead, His Father quickening Him, even as after the same manner His Father will so raise us who believe in Him by Christ Jesus, apart from whom we do not possess the true life" (Ignatius, *To the Trallians* 9; similarly, *To the Smyrnaeans* 1).

As we read these words, we see that Ignatius is placing these events "firmly in the realm of history."[9] We can also see theological consistency with Paul's teaching regarding Jesus' resurrection as being the model for those who believe in him (e.g., Rom 8:11; 1 Cor 6:14; 2 Cor 4:14; Phil 3:20-21; 1 Thess 4:14; etc.).[10]

Similar to Clement, there are references of Peter and Paul as those who were part of the same unified gospel message. For example, while Ignatius is requesting that the church in Rome avoid trying to prevent his execution, he points out that he is not like Peter and Paul, issuing commandments (Ignatius, *To the Romans* 4).[11] Thus, again, there was no deep discord between what the two of them were preaching.[12]

---

[9]Gary R. Habermas, *The Historical Jesus: Ancient Evidence for the Life of Christ* (Joplin, MO: College Press, 1996), 233.

[10]Another area that sounds very similar to Paul in 1 Cor 15:32 is Ignatius, *To the Trallians* 11, where he writes, "But if, as some that are without God, that is, the unbelieving, say, that He only seemed to suffer (they themselves only seeming to exist), then why am I in bonds? Why do I long to be exposed to the wild beasts? Do I therefore die in vain? Am I not then guilty of falsehood against [the cross of] the Lord?"

[11]Ignatius also references Paul in *To the Ephesians* 12.

[12]This is particularly important since, as church historian Bryan Litfin notes, there were challenges of legalism in Antioch that led to Paul having to confront Peter (Gal 2:11-21). See Litfin, *Getting to Know the Church Fathers: An Evangelical Introduction* (Grand Rapids, MI: Brazos, 2007), 35. As bishop of Antioch, Ignatius was in a position to have known,

Ignatius also describes the courage bestowed on Peter and the other disciples such that they became willing to suffer and die: "When, for instance, He came to those who were with Peter, He said to them, 'Lay hold, handle Me, and see that I am not an incorporeal spirit.' And immediately they touched Him, and believed, being convinced both by His flesh and spirit. For this cause also they despised death, and were found its conquerors" (Ignatius, *To the Smyrnaeans* 3; see Lk 24:38-39). Ignatius's statement that the apostles "despised death" is particularly moving. It is one thing to not fear death but another to despise it all together (see 1 Cor 15:54-57). As with Clement, this comment also illustrates the genuineness of the apostles and their beliefs. In the words of Mike Licona, "Liars make poor martyrs."[13]

Ignatius thus provides helpful and early writings that corroborate the NT. It is important to also understand the context in which he was writing. As Justo González points out, "One should not expect that these seven epistles of Ignatius, written within such a brief period under such great pressures, would be detailed, balanced, and systematic expositions of his theology."[14] Despite such a setting, scholars such as Gary Habermas identify several points of contact between his writings and the historical Jesus (and early church).[15] Moreover, these writings are a "welcome enlightenment as to the internal conditions of early Christian communities. They give us a glimpse, too, into the very heart of the great bishop-martyr and breathe forth a profound religious enthusiasm that catches us up and fires us."[16]

---

and he, among others, gives *no indication* that this disagreement led to any sort of civil war within Christianity. Rather, the issue was one that appears to have been resolved, as with other confrontations (e.g., Paul and John Mark).

[13]Michael R. Licona, *The Resurrection of Jesus: A New Historiographical Approach* (Downers Grove, IL: IVP Academic, 2010), 370; Gary R. Habermas and Michael Licona, *The Case for the Resurrection of Jesus* (Grand Rapids, MI: Kregel, 2004), 213, 224.

[14]Justo L. González, *A History of Christian Thought: From the Beginnings to the Council of Chalcedon*, 2nd rev. ed. (Nashville: Abingdon, 1970), 1:73.

[15]Habermas, *Historical Jesus*, 231-33. Habermas identifies eighteen areas within the letters of Ignatius that are relevant for the study of Jesus. He applies a similar systematic approach to other early Christian and non-Christian writings outside the NT.

[16]Quasten, *Patrology* 1:64.

POLYCARP OF SMYRNA

Irenaeus of Lyons (ca. AD 130–200) provides some details about the life of Polycarp. He states that Polycarp was "instructed by apostles . . . but was also, by apostles in Asia, appointed bishop of the Church in Smyrna" and furthermore that Polycarp knew the apostle John (Irenaeus, *Against Heresies* 3.3.4; Eusebius, *Ecclesiastical History* 5.20.5-6).[17] Irenaeus states that Polycarp wrote multiple letters, but the only one that remains is his letter to the church in Philippi.

The church in Philippi asked Polycarp to send a copy of the letters of Ignatius (recall that one of Ignatius's letters was written to Polycarp). Polycarp sent Ignatius's letters along with a short letter of his own in the early second century.[18] Though Polycarp knew John and his letter covers various topics, its value for our purposes is its discussion of Paul and references to the New Testament writings.

Concerning Paul, we find Polycarp telling the Philippians (a church to which Paul had already written a letter) the following: "For neither I, nor any other such one, can come up to the wisdom of the blessed and glorified Paul. . . . He wrote you a letter, which, if you carefully study, you will find to be the means of building you up in that faith which has been given you" (*To the Philippians* 3; see also 10). Later he encourages the church to follow the examples of Ignatius "and in Paul himself, and the rest of the apostles. [This do] in assurance that all these have not run in vain, but in faith and righteousness, and that they are [now] in their due place in the presence of the Lord, with whom also they suffered. For they loved not this present world, but Him who died for us, and for our sakes was raised again by God from the dead" (*To the Philippians* 9).

Paul, Ignatius, and others were willing to suffer and die for the gospel. Part of the reason for this is that they did not love the present world and were ready to suffer and die, knowing that death was not the end. For they would be in the presence of the Lord (see Phil 1:23)

[17]We can note that Irenaeus states his own connection to Polycarp as well.

[18]Polycarp's letter might be two letters combined. See Quasten, *Patrology* 1:80; González, *History of Christian Thought* 1:80-81.

and were looking forward to a future resurrection (Polycarp, *To the Philippians* 5).

Another essential part of Polycarp's letter is that "it seems to reflect all the Pauline epistles but Philemon, as well as 1 or 2 John, 1 Peter, 1 Clement, some of the Ignatian letters, Synoptic traditions, and perhaps Acts, James, and Hermas."[19] This is a significant number of references in a letter that is only about four pages long. While it can be difficult to discern all of the letter's quotations, allusions, and influences, Polycarp identifies Ephesians 4:26 as being a part of the "Scriptures" (*To the Philippians* 12).

CONCLUSION

There are a number of other early noncanonical Christian sources I could have mentioned here, such as Papias, the Didache, the Epistle of Barnabas, the Shepherd of Hermas, Quadratus, Justin Martyr, Irenaeus of Lyons, and others. I decided to present Clement, Ignatius, and Polycarp as three representatives that illustrate how early church writings corroborate various components of the New Testament. As with the non-Christian sources, these sources provide yet another angle that adds to the reliability of the New Testament texts.

KEY TAKEAWAYS: NONCANONICAL CHRISTIAN SOURCES

- Noncanonical Christian sources are those not found in the New Testament. Many of these sources are nevertheless early and provide valuable insight into early Christianity.
- There are several early noncanonical Christian sources. I mentioned Clement of Rome, Ignatius of Antioch, and Polycarp of Smyrna.
- These sources, as with the non-Christian sources, further corroborate information in the New Testament writings.

[19]Robert M. Grant, *The Apostolic Fathers: A New Translation and Commentary*, vol. 1, *An Introduction* (New York: Thomas Nelson and Sons, 1964), 66.

RECOMMENDED READING

González, Justo L. *A History of Christian Thought: From the Beginnings to the Council of Chalcedon*. Vol. 1. 2nd rev. ed. Nashville: Abingdon, 1987.

Litfin, Bryan M. *Getting to Know the Church Fathers: An Evangelical Introduction*. Grand Rapids, MI: Brazos, 2007.

Shelley, Bruce. *Church History in Plain Language*. 3rd ed. Nashville: Thomas Nelson, 2008.

11

NEW TESTAMENT CANON AND CREDIBILITY

The word *canon* can refer to a straight rod or stick that may be used as a standard. So when I refer to the New Testament canon, I am referring to the twenty-seven books of the New Testament as being a standard. But what kind of standard? Are they a historical standard that accurately reflects the words and deeds of Jesus and the early church? Well, in many ways, yes.[1] Do they provide a theological and/or spiritual standard? Again, the answer here is yes. While our focus thus far has primarily been historical, in this chapter we will see that separating history and theology is not always so easy.[2]

When it comes to the New Testament canon, renowned Princeton scholar Bruce Metzger states that the "knowledge that our New Testament contains the best sources for the history of Jesus is the most valuable knowledge that can be obtained from the study of the early history of the canon. In fact . . . it is certain that those who discerned the limits of the canon had a clear and balanced perception of the

---

[1]This is *not* to say that sources outside the NT are of no historical value. Several prior chapters, as well as this one, demonstrate why the NT books are good historical sources.

[2]Despite what some scholars today think, history and theology are not mutually exclusive. Jesus' death, for example, is a historical event with theological significance. Additionally, different definitions or understandings of canon can affect one's conclusions. See Michael J. Kruger, *The Question of Canon: Challenging the Status Quo in the New Testament Debate* (Downers Grove, IL: IVP Academic, 2013), 45-46 (noting exclusive, functional, and ontological definitions).

gospel of Jesus Christ."[3] In other words, if you want the best sources for learning about Jesus, look to the New Testament.

This chapter will briefly highlight some aspects of how the New Testament was formed to help illustrate Metzger's point. In doing so, we will look at the canon's development and at books that were accepted and rejected. Accordingly, this chapter will provide a zoomed-out view of reliability. As we will see, it is in some ways a return to the beginning chapters of this book.

CRITERIA FOR THE CANON?

Let us start with a quick thought experiment as we begin discussing how the New Testament was formed. Pretend for a moment that you are in the early church and want to find out which Christian writings are reliable and authoritative and which are not. As someone who cares about knowing the truth about Jesus and the gospel, you are faced with several works circulating at the time. Each purports to tell you about Jesus and/or the early church. Now, what are you going to do? How will you figure out which sources are reliable and which are not? Do you have any criteria that help you decide? What are they?

Hopefully this book has already provided you with some initial answers. One thing we would want would be to have sources that were written as close as possible to the events themselves (e.g., dating). Additionally, we would want sources that were written by the apostles or someone associated the apostles (authorship). Each of these two criteria seems quite intuitive and obvious. Indeed, we naturally considered them at the outset of this book.

Other criteria for canonicity have also been suggested.[4] For example, widespread acceptance and usage of a writing was also an important

---

[3]Bruce M. Metzger, *The Canon of the New Testament: Its Origin, Development, and Significance* (Oxford: Clarendon, 1997), 287.

[4]For three lists of criteria that each slightly differ from one another, see F. F. Bruce, *The Canon of Scripture* (Downers Grove, IL: IVP Academic, 1988), 256-68; Metzger, *Canon of the New Testament*, 251-54; Lee Martin McDonald, *The Biblical Canon: Its Origin, Transmission, and Authority* (Peabody, MA: Hendrickson, 2007), 406-20.

factor.[5] Works that were only recognized in small, localized areas were less likely to be authoritative for the whole church (see Clement below).[6] Additionally, the teachings of the works would need to be consistent with what the apostles taught in the churches they founded.

We can see why these criteria guided how the New Testament canon developed. Helpful though they may be, some refinement is in order. While the criteria provide a useful framework for understanding the canon, we need to remember that it would be anachronistic to say that the early church went around *looking for* reliable writings. Rather, they *already had* writings they believed were reliable (to varying degrees). In other words, these criteria were the "church's attempt to explain what it *already* had, rather than a process of *deciding* what to have."[7] Thus these reasonable criteria provide just one angle for understanding the New Testament canon.[8] Although they were helpful, as Metzger notes, "the Church did not create the canon but came to recognize, accept, affirm, and confirm the self-authenticating quality of certain documents that imposed themselves as such upon the church. If this fact is obscured, one comes into serious conflict not with dogma but with history."[9]

With these comments in mind, we can see that these criteria make sense because we would expect to find teachings *different* from the apostles in an isolated, local territory. Why? Because it would be highly improbable for the same distortion to occur throughout several churches in other regions simultaneously and independently.

---

[5]Lee McDonald suggests that the "widespread use of the NT writings in the churches may have been the most determinative factor in the canonical process" (*Biblical Canon*, 414). However, Michael Kruger suggests that "the apostolicity of a book has emerged as the primary or dominant one." See Kruger, *Canon Revisited: Establishing the Origins and Authority of the New Testament Books* (Wheaton, IL: Crossway, 2012), 75.

[6]It should be clear that letters would naturally start with local acceptance before receiving a wider acceptance. It would take time for letters to be copied, be transported to new locations, be read, and so on.

[7]Kruger, *Canon Revisited*, 82, emphasis original. He agrees that they are helpful and that "the evidential case put forth by the criteria-of-canonicity model is strong and ought to be used in our defense of the canon" (81).

[8]For a helpful discussion on the role of the Holy Spirit, see Kruger, *Canon Revisited*, 88-122.

[9]Metzger, *Canon of the New Testament*, 287.

Divergent teachings would soon confront the teachings of the universal church. One of the tools used to challenge such teachings would be to appeal to the apostles' teachings.[10] The apostles were those who were in the best position (historically) to know what Jesus said and did, and they were also (theologically) empowered by the Holy Spirit in sharing this message (Lk 12:12; Jn 14:26).

The early church recognized these connections. For example, Clement of Rome (ca. AD 90) comments, "The apostles were given the gospel for us by the Lord Jesus Christ, and Jesus Christ was sent forth from God. Thus Christ came from God and the apostles from Christ" (1 Clement 42.1-2; see Eph 2:20).[11] Likewise, Justin Martyr (ca. AD 150) frequently refers to the "memoirs of the apostles" and states, "The apostles in the memoirs composed by them, which are called Gospels, have thus delivered unto us what was enjoined upon them" (*Dialogue with Trypho* 66).[12] Indeed, after the initial followers of Jesus began to die and their writings circulated, others in the first and second centuries recognized the authoritative nature of their writings and the need to preserve them.[13]

EUSEBIUS'S FOUR CATEGORIES

During the first centuries after Jesus' death, a few factors came together to create a greater need for a standard or canon of Christian writings. Eusebius of Caesarea was an early church historian who wrote *Church History* (also known as *Ecclesiastical History*) around AD 320. This

[10]It would be idealistic to assume that Christians would always and boldly stand against false teachings (see Gal 1:6).

[11]LCL 24.

[12]In the next chapter Justin says that these memoirs are read along with the prophets when believers come together to meet on Sundays. There thus appears a connection with OT Scriptures.

[13]After examining several other first- and second-century church comments (such as from Ignatius, Didache, Papias, Epistle of Barnabas, Polycarp, Shepherd of Hermas, and others), Metzger concludes that these accounts demonstrate that an authority was sensed in the church before any theories had developed (*Canon of the New Testament*, 73; see also 40-72). Kruger comments on the importance of their teachings getting a permanent form (*Question of Canon*, 71).

work contains one of the earliest lists of accepted Christian writings.[14] Eusebius describes various Christian writings along with some comments about how Christians viewed them. Notably, in his own assessment, he gives four different categories of writings: accepted, disputed, spurious, and heretical (*Ecclesiastical History* 3.25.1-7). We can illustrate the breakdown of these four categories in the following way:[15]

Table 11.1. Categories of early Christian writings

Canonical	Noncanonical
Recognized writings	Spurious (helpful, but not Scripture)
Disputed writings	Heretical

Using his classifications will help us to further understand why some books were included in the New Testament canon and why others were excluded.

Canonical. Books that were eventually included in the canon were either accepted all along by the church or initially disputed by some.

Accepted. Some books were widely and readily accepted. Included in these writings are the Gospels, Acts, and Paul's letters (which, for Eusebius, includes Hebrews).[16] In addition to these writings, Eusebius mentions the first epistles of Peter and John. He then closes with Revelation as the final book to be included, though noting that there were some differing opinions.[17] This first group, then, includes twenty-two books of the New Testament. We have seen throughout the present book that the Gospels, Acts, and Paul's letters are particularly reliable, and it should be unsurprising that the early church recognized this as well. For Eusebius, these books are "acknowledged as genuine" (*Ecclesiastical History* 3.25.3).

[14]The Muratorian Fragment is another, even earlier, list.

[15]For other helpful illustrations see Metzger, *Canon of the New Testament*, 205; Kruger, *Canon Revisited*, 268.

[16]For fourteen total letters (Eusebius, *Ecclesiastical History* 3.3.5).

[17]Revelation is included in this section with some curious comments that are made more perplexing by the fact that he includes this work in the spurious writings as well. Note, however, that there are other apocalypses noted in the spurious section.

Disputed. Eusebius then moves to books he considers disputed, "though they are known and approved by many" (*Ecclesiastical History* 3.25.3).[18] The five books he lists are James, Jude, 2 Peter, and 2 and 3 John. Elsewhere Eusebius notes that James and Jude are among the epistles of the universal church and are "publicly used in most of the churches" (*Ecclesiastical History* 2.23.25). Thus, although there were some questions regarding these books, they were in fact widely used and well known. They complete the New Testament canon when included in the list above. There are, then, a total of twenty-seven books when we combine the twenty-two accepted books with the five disputed books.[19]

Table 11.2. Subcategories of canonical writings

Canonical	
Recognized	**Disputed**
Gospels Acts Paul's Writings (14, including Hebrews) 1 Peter 1 John Revelation	James Jude 2 Peter 2 John 3 John

Noncanonical. Not all books outside the canon fall into the same category because some were considered helpful and others were considered heretical.

Spurious. The next set of books were considered helpful but not on the same level as Scripture. These works included the Acts of Paul, Shepherd of Hermas, Apocalypse of Peter, Epistle of Barnabas, Teachings of the Apostles (also known as the Didache), and Gospel of the Hebrews. While each writing had a differing level of usefulness in the churches, of these writings perhaps the most popular were the Shepherd of Hermas, Epistle of Barnabas, and Teachings of the Apostles.

What is interesting about these writings is that although they are noncanonical, they remain useful for us to consider. They illustrate that

[18]Compare with Metzger's "nevertheless familiar to the majority" translation in *Canon of the New Testament*, 309.

[19]For a brief analysis of these books see Kruger, *Canon Revisited*, 269-74.

meeting one (or more) of the above criteria was not always sufficient to include a book in the canon.[20] Clement's letter to Corinth, for example, was written during the time of the apostles and by someone who was associated with the apostles (Phil 4:3) but was *never* canonized (see Eusebius, *Ecclesiastical History* 3.16.1, 3.39.1). The letter was considered beneficial to read, especially in Corinth, but not on the same level as Scripture. With works like these being excluded from the New Testament canon, even though they were considered helpful, we see a general practice of excluding books rather than uncritical acceptance. Despite their popularity, even writings like the Shepherd of Hermas or the Epistle to Barnabas were not considered to have the same authoritative status as others.

Rejected. We now turn to the final section, where most questions are raised today. In this category, Eusebius includes writings "by the heretics under the name of the apostles," which include the Gospel of Peter, Gospel of Thomas, and the Gospel of Matthias, while the Acts of Andrew, Acts of John, and the acts of "others" are also mentioned.[21] Why were these books rejected? Why were they, in Eusebius's words, considered "rejected as altogether absurd and impious" (*Ecclesiastical History* 3.25.7)?

Let us look briefly at the Gospel of Thomas since it is one of the most discussed of the noncanonical Gospels. First, Eusebius notes that works like this have a different "character" from those mentioned above and that they deviate "as far as possible from sound orthodoxy" (*Ecclesiastical History* 3.25.7).[22] This is evident in considering the text itself. Unlike the New Testament Gospels, Thomas is a sayings document that records various sayings of Jesus.

What does Thomas write concerning the words of Jesus? Perhaps the last saying in Thomas (logion 114) is the most notable. It says,

---

[20]As also noted by Kruger, *Canon Revisited*, 82.

[21]Eusebius, *Ecclesiastical History*, 3.25.6.

[22]Indeed, in the prologue to Thomas, it states that what is about to be presented are the "secret" teachings of Jesus. Presumably this indicates the author's intention to convey information unknown elsewhere, which is also consistent with various Gnostic groups that appealed to secret knowledge.

"Simon Peter said to them, 'Let Mary come out from us, because women are not worthy of life.' Jesus said, 'Behold, I will draw her so that I might make her male, so that she also might be a living spirit resembling you males. For every woman who makes herself male will enter the kingdom of God.'"[23] This seems quite different from Jesus' words in Mark 3:35, where those who do the will of God are Jesus' "brother, and sister, and mother."[24] It also seems quite different from Paul's teachings in Galatians 3:28, where there is "neither male nor female; for you are all one in Christ Jesus." Similar language is also used in Romans 10:9-13, where Paul discusses salvation.

Second, this work was written far too late to have been actually written by Jesus' disciple Thomas. Simon Gathercole has done a detailed study on Thomas and concludes that it was written sometime around AD 135–200.[25] It seems that Thomas's name was attached to this writing to make the "secret" teachings within this work appear more authoritative.

Accordingly, Thomas, like the other works mentioned by Eusebius, was widely rejected. "It is not surprising," Kruger writes, "that *Thomas* is never mentioned in any early canonical list, is not found in any of our New Testament manuscript collections, never figured prominently in canonical discussions, and was often condemned outright by a variety of church fathers."[26] This is not just a theological point but also a historical one, since Thomas is not often regarded as very useful in historical investigations into Jesus' life.[27]

---

[23]Translation by Simon Gathercole, *The Gospel of Thomas: Introduction and Commentary* (Boston: Brill, 2014), 607.

[24]Moreover, one might note that it is the women who are reported to have found the empty tomb in the NT Gospels.

[25]Gathercole, *Gospel of Thomas*, 121, 124. Gathercole also notes that although Thomas could not be the author, its original author is unknown (124). Virtually nobody holds that Jesus' disciple Thomas actually wrote this work.

[26]Kruger, *Canon Revisited*, 278.

[27]Gathercole, *Gospel of Thomas*, 184. "As scholarship currently stands, and with the primary sources that are available to us at present, the *Gospel of Thomas* can hardly be regarded as useful in the reconstruction of a historical picture of Jesus."

Table 11.3. Subcategories of noncanonical writings

Noncanonical	
Spurious	**Rejected**
Acts of Paul Shepherd of Hermas Apocalypse of Peter Epistle of Barnabas Teachings of the Apostles (Didache) Gospel of the Hebrews	Gospel of Peter Gospel of Thomas Gospel of Matthias[a] Acts of Andrew Acts of John "Others"

[a]As F. F. Bruce notes, Origen recognized the Gospel of Matthias as a heretical writing (*Homilies on Luke 1*). See Bruce, *The Canon of Scripture* (Downers Grove, IL: IVP Academic, 1988), 201. Eusebius's reference here is clearly not to the canonical Gospel of Matthew, since he earlier references the four Gospels as accepted in this chapter and elsewhere in his work.

CONCLUSION

We have seen some initial reasons why the New Testament canon is a reliable collection of books. It is not the fault of believers that the early church collected the best and most reliable sources. As Bart Ehrman writes, "Whatever one thinks of them as inspired scripture, they can be seen and used as significant historical sources."[28]

We started this chapter with Ehrman's professor Bruce Metzger and his comments regarding the strength of the canon's reliability. After having been introduced to a sampling of these issues, we might now agree with him that "one can say with even greater assurance than before that no books or collections of books from the ancient Church may be compared with the New Testament in importance for Christian history or doctrine."[29]

[28]Bart D. Ehrman, *Did Jesus Exist? The Historical Argument for Jesus of Nazareth* (New York: HarperOne, 2012), 74; see also 259-63. Also, as I noted in chapter three, Ehrman also points out that almost all of the Christian writings we have that can confidently be dated to the first century are those within the NT (an example of an exception would be Clement of Rome). See Ehrman, *The New Testament: A Historical Introduction to the Early Christian Writings*, 7th ed. (New York: Oxford University Press, 2019), 6.

[29]Metzger, *Canon of the New Testament*, 287.

KEY TAKEAWAYS: NEW TESTAMENT CANON

- From a historically reliable perspective, the sources collected by the early church and put into the New Testament canon (or "standard") are the best sources we have. As Metzger argues, nothing compares to the New Testament canon, as it consists of the "best sources."
- Just like in other areas of history, various criteria help us understand why some books were included, others were considered, and still others were rejected. These criteria offer a helpful framework for understanding the canon and include being associated with an apostle, being written during the right time, having widespread agreement/use, and so on.
- Eusebius provides some important information regarding the views of the early church and the formation of the New Testament canon.

RECOMMENDED READING

Bruce, F. F. *The Canon of Scripture*. Downers Grove, IL: IVP Academic, 1988.

Laird, Benjamin P. *Creating the Canon: Composition, Controversy, and the Authority of the New Testament*. Downers Grove, IL: IVP Academic, 2023.

Kruger, Michael J. *The Question of Canon: Challenging the Status Quo in the New Testament Debate*. Downers Grove, IL: IVP Academic, 2013.

12

SPIRITUAL AND LIFE TRANSFORMATION

While the prior considerations typically dealt with ancient evidence, this chapter focuses on past *and* present data. The reason for this is that if the radical teachings of the New Testament are true, then we would expect to see their impact on the lives of individuals. Indeed, it would be a strange thing if the New Testament was completely true and there were *no* substantive impact in the world. In other words, if Jesus was who he said he was and his subsequent followers were filled with the power and presence of the Holy Spirit, we would expect to find people, families, communities, and countries transformed. Is this what we find? In this chapter, I will briefly highlight examples of believers and nonbelievers testifying to the transformative effects of the New Testament.

To be clear, I am *not* arguing that simply because a book has made an impact, it is reliable, *nor* am I saying that transformation equals trustworthiness. I want to stress that the argument here is one of consistency. Clearly, a book could have an impact and be false, untrustworthy, unreliable, and so on.[1] Effect or impact does not *confer* trustworthiness but is *consistent* with it. The point here is that if the *New Testament teachings specifically* are true, then individuals and communities will feel their effects.

---

[1]Various religious, philosophical, and political texts have clearly made an impact, but that alone does not mean that they are therefore trustworthy.

A final point worth noting is that while the other aspects of reliability we have examined typically focus on zoomed-in or zoomed-out aspects, this aspect has to do with the one holding the map. When seeing the map, one may recognize more than just the roads and mountains but also the beauty of a kingdom in the map. Perhaps there is such beauty in the map that the one looking at the map has decided to go to the kingdom depicted and become a citizen (like in *The Pilgrim's Progress*). Others may see the same kingdom on the map and think it provides a nice picture but are, for one reason or another, uninterested in going there or becoming citizens. The point is that in this chapter I will identify transformed lives that are, as noted above, consistent with the New Testament being reliable.

DIRECT IMPACT (BELIEVERS)

Several New Testament texts affirm that people will be directly affected personally by its message. The truths of the New Testament are not merely abstract truths unconnected from the real world, nor are they merely intellectual truths for us to simply agree to (see Jas 2:19). Rather, as Hebrews 4:12 states, "The word of God is living and active, and sharper than any two-edged sword, even penetrating as far as the division of soul and spirit, of both joints and marrow, and able to judge the thoughts and intentions of the heart" (see also Jn 14–16 and 2 Tim 3:16-17). Within the New Testament, there are truths that confront not only the mind but also the heart, soul, and strength of a person.

For example, when the New Testament speaks about sin, judgment, and immorality, this prompts readers to assess their own morality, including moral failings. Several psychological, philosophical, and historical studies recognize humanity's overly optimistic moral evaluations.[2] Justin Tosi and Brandon Warmke point out, "Decades of research on moral

[2]See comments and studies mentioned by philosophers Justin Tosi and Brandon Warmke, *Grandstanding: The Use and Abuse of Moral Talk* (New York: Oxford University Press, 2020), 23-26, 106-7. Other studies include Carol Tavris and Elliot Aronson, *Mistakes Were Made (but Not By Me): Why We Justify Foolish Beliefs, Bad Decisions, and Hurtful Acts*, 3rd repr. ed. (Boston Mariner Books, 2020); Christopher R. Browning, *Ordinary Men: Reserve Police Battalion 101 and the Final Solution in Poland*, rev. ed. (New York: HarperCollins,

character suggest that we aren't as virtuous as we think we are."[3] Self-righteousness is a temptation we are all confronted with. Despite the fact we often think of ourselves as "good" or more moral than most, we are faced with a different reality and moral standard in the New Testament. As we read the Sermon on the Mount (Mt 5–7, esp. Mt 7:1-5), our self-proclaimed self-righteousness is confronted by what Jesus did and taught.

Indeed, although we may frequently overestimate our moral goodness, we can nevertheless recognize our moral shortcomings and wrestle with feelings of guilt.[4] While not everyone follows Jesus, the focus here is on those who have been directly convicted and subsequently committed themselves to Jesus.[5]

Augustine of Hippo (AD 354–430) is a helpful example of such a person. Augustine was a promiscuous pagan who had several worldly struggles. One day, as Augustine was in a garden wrestling with sin and temptation, he heard the voice of a child say, "Tolle lege, tolle lege" ("Take it and read, take it and read"). At this comment, Augustine picked up one of Paul's writings, and the first thing he read was from Romans 13:13-14: "Let's behave properly as in the day, not in carousing and drunkenness, not in sexual promiscuity and debauchery, not in strife and jealousy. But put on the Lord Jesus Christ, and make no provision for the flesh in regard to its lusts." Upon reading these words, Augustine comments, "I had no wish to read more and no need to do so. For in an instant as I came to the end of the sentence, it was as though the light of confidence flooded into my heart and all the darkness of doubt was dispelled."[6]

2017). The importance of the last study by Browning is that the Nazis did not go around collecting "bad people"; rather they simply used ordinary men.

[3]Tosi and Warmke, *Grandstanding*, 25.

[4]See Jn 16:8, which says that the Holy Spirit ("helper") will come to "convict the world regarding sin, and righteousness, and judgment." Tosi and Warmke also note that people often try to assuage guilt and moral reputation (*Grandstanding*, 25-26, 60, 102-3). Since forgiveness is not mentioned in their book, it is helpful to compare these concerns with the NT teachings of forgiveness as graciously offered through Jesus (e.g., Acts 3:19; Rom 3:24-25; Eph 1:7; 2:1-10).

[5]Where this confrontation or conviction leads will vary (see Mt 13:3-9, 18-23).

[6]Saint Augustine, *Confessions*, trans. R. S. Pine-Coffin (Baltimore: Penguin Books, 1961), 178.

Peter Hitchens, brother of the late atheist Christopher Hitchens, relates a somewhat similar experience. Though he grew up in a Christian environment, he strongly rebelled against it, to the point of even setting his Bible on fire. However, after becoming disillusioned with his rebellion, he came across Rogier van der Weyden's portrait of *The Last Judgment*. Hitchens's reaction to this image was, "I had a sudden and strong sense of religion being a thing of present day, not imprisoned under thick layers of time. A large catalogue of misdeeds . . . replayed themselves rapidly in my head." Hitchens realized he stood condemned for his immorality and was confronted with a strange fact he had been unaware of until that point. Specifically, he had "no idea that an adult could be frightened, in broad daylight and after a good lunch, by such things." Yet, he goes on to argue that such a fear was proper and can be "an important gift that helps us to think clearly at moments of danger."[7] The conviction of his sin and fear of judgment led him to repent and turn to Jesus for forgiveness, such that his life was radically transformed.

Augustine and Hitchens each had an experience that appears to have encompassed more than just their mind but the entirety of their being. Such transformations (i.e., conversion and commitment to Christ) led to changes in their thinking and actions. In fact, immediately after referring to the gospel message, Paul states in Ephesians 2:10, "For we are His workmanship, created in Christ Jesus for good works, which God prepared beforehand so that we would walk in them." Believers are now a "new creation" in Jesus to do the will of God by walking in the good works prepared for us.[8]

Vishal Mangalwadi is a Christian from India who became a believer, in part, by reading the Bible. He was struck by the impartiality found within the Bible, particularly the Old Testament. He comments, "Literature is something we interpret. Revelation [the Bible] also

---

[7]Peter Hitchens, *The Rage Against God: How Atheism Led Me to Faith* (Grand Rapids, MI: Zondervan, 2010), 17, 103; see Prov 1:7.

[8]That we are a "new creation" is found in 2 Cor 5:17; Gal 6:15, while putting on Jesus is found in several verses (Rom 13:12-14; Eph 4:24; etc.). Particularly helpful here is Anthony C. Thornhill, "The Resurrection of Jesus and Spiritual (Trans)Formation," *Journal of Spiritual Formation and Soul Care* 5, no. 2 (2012): 243-56.

interprets and evaluates us. It stands above us, judges us, and calls us back to sanity."[9] He read more and more about the God of the Bible before asking whether this God was in fact seeking to bless the nations, especially India.

What answer did Mangalwadi find to his question? He writes the following:

> My investigation of whether God had truly blessed India through the Bible yielded incredible discoveries: the university . . . the municipality and democracy . . . the High Court . . . the legal system . . . the modern Hindi that I spoke . . . the secular newspaper . . . the army cantonment . . . the botanical garden . . . the public library . . . the railway . . . the medical system I depended on, the Agricultural Institute across town—*all of these came to my city because some people took the Bible seriously*.[10]

Throughout his work, Mangalwadi identifies several missionaries, reformers, scientists, and others who were dramatically transformed because of the gospel. He provides helpful examples and accounts of how these blessings were manifested through the love and efforts of believers. We should add Mangalwadi to this list as well, since he was himself arrested for trying to help poor farmers whose crops had been destroyed by a hailstorm.[11]

These are just a few accounts of those who experienced a direct encounter with the teachings of the New Testament. Each was led to repentance and commitment to Jesus. Commitment to Jesus led them to grow in Christ as a new creation by putting on "a heart of compassion, kindness, humility, gentleness and patience . . . [and in] addition to all these things . . . love" (Col 3:12, 14).[12]

---

[9]Vishal Mangalwadi, *The Book That Made Your World: How the Bible Created the Soul of Western Civilization* (Nashville: Thomas Nelson, 2011), 54.

[10]Mangalwadi, *Book That Made Your World*, 55, emphasis added.

[11]Mangalwadi, *Book That Made Your World*, 31-37.

[12]Again, I want to stress that I am arguing that these individuals' being transformed because of the NT message is consistent with that message being true. I am not arguing it is true because people were changed. Again, it is not conferring truth but is consistent with it.

INDIRECT IMPACT

If believers claim to have experienced the *direct* impact of the New Testament personally and experientially, agnostics and skeptics have been *indirectly* affected in some way as well. The focus here is on how nonbelievers can see how the New Testament teachings have affected those around them, not whether they have had these experiences themselves. In other words, even those who are not Christians have indirectly recognized and experienced the change in others caused by the teachings of the New Testament.[13]

There is a broad spectrum of labels that non-Christians can hold. Accordingly, I will not try to label these thinkers except to note that they have not made any explicit commitment to Jesus (Rom 10:9-13) that I am presently aware. Rather, they appear to respect aspects of Christianity in one way or another.

One quite surprising person who recently made some positive remarks is prominent atheist Richard Dawkins. In 2019, he wrote, "It does unfortunately seem plausible that, if somebody sincerely believes God is watching his every move, he might be more likely to be good."[14] This comment was in response to a recent experiment that involved an honesty box and decisively concluded that those who believed someone was watching acted more honestly than those who did not.

For Dawkins, this confirmed that most people are far less honest than he thought or even wanted to think. He writes, "I must say that I hate that idea. I want to believe that humans are better than that. I'd like to believe that we are honest whether anyone is watching or not."[15]

---

[13]Justin Brierley, *The Surprising Rebirth of Belief in God: Why New Atheism Grew Old and Secular Thinkers Are Considering Christianity Again* (Carol Stream, IL: Tyndale Elevate, 2023).

[14]Richard Dawkins, *Outgrowing God: A Beginner's Guide* (NY: Random House, 2019), 99. Dawkins is referring to a God like the one in Christianity but is not referring exclusively to the Christian religion here.

[15]Dawkins, *Outgrowing God*, 99. Dawkins is not referring exclusively to the Christian religion here. It is worth noting that Dawkins scoffs at the idea that fear should play a role in morality (96-98). As noted above, Peter Hitchens saw fear as a gift of clear thinking and recognized its value in restraining evil, even in his own life. He acknowledges, "I faced a private moral dilemma in which fear of doing an evil thing held me back from doing it, for which I remain immeasurably glad" (*Rage Against God*, 104-5).

Yet as we saw above and across multiple disciplines, people overstate their moral goodness, and we ought not to be as optimistic regarding our morality as we, or Dawkins, think. In any event, Dawkins's views are presented even more provocatively in an article titled, "Ending Religion Is a Bad Idea, Says Richard Dawkins."[16]

Tom Holland, an agnostic historian (*not* Spider-Man), recently wrote a large history of the Western world called *Dominion: How the Christian Revolution Remade the World*. In this work, he acknowledges that although he grew up in a Christian home, his faith had been diminished to the point that he was reluctant even to think that his values, and those generally present in the West, "might be traceable to Christian origins."[17] He shares his fascination with famed leaders from Greece (Leonidas) and Rome (Caesar), believing that his values were likely derived from these sources much more so than anything Christianity ever offered.

However, he describes how the alternative he found to Christianity was much more frightening. He writes,

> The more years I spent immersed in the study of classical antiquity, so the more alien I increasingly found it. The values of Leonidas, whose people had practiced a peculiarly murderous form of eugenics and trained their young to kill . . . were nothing that I recognised as my own; nor were those of Caesar, who was reported to have killed a million Gauls, and enslaved a million more. It was not just the extreme of callousness that unsettled me, but the complete lack of any sense that the poor or weak might have the slightest intrinsic value. Why did I find this disturbing? Because, in my morals and ethics, I was not a Spartan or a Roman at all.[18]

Holland recognized that his values were not those of the ancient Greco-Roman world but those of a civilization that had distinctly Christian

---

[16]David Sanderson, "Ending Religion Is a Bad Idea, Says Richard Dawkins," *The Times*, October 5, 2019, www.thetimes.co.uk/article/ending-religion-is-a-bad-idea-says-richard-dawkins-sqqdbmcpq.

[17]Tom Holland, *Dominion: How the Christian Revolution Remade the World* (New York: Basic Books, 2019), 15. He notes that he had only "vaguely continued to believe in God."

[18]Holland, *Dominion*, 16-17.

roots. One reason for this is how Jesus' death on the cross challenged the authorities of that day and instilled intrinsic value on all of humanity.[19] Throughout the work, Holland identifies a wide variety of valuable contributions of Christianity throughout Western society (socially, scientifically, etc.).[20]

AUTHENTIC CHRISTIANITY

Bart Ehrman, an atheist/agnostic New Testament scholar, states, "Anyone who follows such teachings [e.g., Sermon on the Mount] is obviously going to do real service to the human race and work to make society better."[21] While he recognizes how genuine believers contribute positively to society, Ehrman then goes on to highlight others that have used Christianity to justify evil actions. While it may seem clear that many of these instances are obvious abuses of Jesus' teachings rather than their logical outworkings, the New Testament itself references the reality of impostors and wolves in sheep's clothing who will pretend to be followers of Jesus (e.g., Mt 7:15-23; 24:24-25; Rom 2:24).

William Lecky (1838–1903) was aware of the issues facing Christianity because of various theological disagreements. While he is often considered a skeptic, he was apparently not an atheist when he wrote his earlier publications.[22] Nevertheless, he provides a particularly strong comment regarding Jesus and authentic Christianity. He writes,

> It was reserved for Christianity to present to the world an ideal character, which through all the changes of eighteen centuries

---

[19]Holland, *Dominion*, 6-12; see also 464, 494-95.

[20]In many ways, Holland's work is simply a longer treatment of Mangalwadi's.

[21]Bart D. Ehrman, *The New Testament: A Historical Introduction to the Early Christian Writings*, 7th ed. (New York: Oxford University Press, 2019), 2. Ehrman sounds very similar to Holland when he states, "If one does not understand the New Testament, one cannot fully understand the course of history of the world we inhabit" (1).

[22]William Edward Hartpole Lecky, *The Religious Tendencies of the Age* (London: Saunders, Otley, 1860), 148. "To disbelieve Christianity is to believe that these things are the result of blind chance. . . . Truly there is no credulity like the credulity of unbelief." Since Lecky was around twenty-two when he wrote this, it is possible that he changed his mind later in life and/or that he was skeptical of more organized forms of Christianity (or religion). See F. F. Bruce, *The New Testament Documents: Are They Reliable?*, 6th ed. (Grand Rapids, MI: Eerdmans, 1981), 3. Bruce states that Lecky was "no believer in revealed religion."

> has inspired the hearts of men with an impassioned love; has shown itself capable of acting on all ages, nations, temperaments, and conditions; has been not only the highest pattern of virtue but the strongest incentive to its practice; and has exercised so deep an influence that it may be truly said that the simple record of three short years of active life has done more to regenerate and to soften mankind than all the disquisitions of philosophers, and all the exhortations of moralists.[23]

Like Holland and others, Lecky recognized the impact that Jesus' life had throughout the next several centuries. Many other philosophers have tried, but none have been able to *soften* humankind with anywhere close to the influence that Jesus has had. Jesus' life, death, and resurrection offer humanity a chance for forgiveness, redemption, and hope.

CONCLUSION

I close this chapter with a reminder that I am *not* arguing that the influence of Christianity confers trustworthiness on it. Instead, its impact is consistent with its trustworthiness. If Christianity is true, we would expect it to have the effects Lecky describes. Yet, as Mangalwadi points out, as we read the New Testament to understand it, its teachings confront and challenge us as well. Millions of people have read these writings, recognized their sin, turned from immorality, and followed Jesus. These *direct* experiences have led to lives so radically transformed that even those around them can *indirectly* attest to the positive change.

KEY TAKEAWAYS: SPIRITUAL AND LIFE TRANSFORMATION

- The power of the New Testament to transform individuals and provide both direct and indirect evidence adds only a very limited level of reliability. The reason for this is that it does not actually *confer* reliability but it is *consistent* with the New

[23]William Edward Hartpole Lecky, *History of European Morals, from Augustus to Charlemagne*, 3rd ed. (New York: D. Appleton, 1897), 2:8-9.

Testament being a reliable source. I am *not* arguing that because people are transformed, the New Testament is reliable.

- Believers may find direct evidence of the reality of the events of Jesus' life in their own lives. Dramatic transformations of both individuals and communities are important.
- Nonbelievers will find indirect evidence insofar as they see the transformation in their family, friends, and communities around them.

RECOMMENDED READING

Holland, Tom. *Dominion: How the Christian Revolution Remade the World.* New York: Basic Books, 2019.

Mangalwadi, Vishal. *The Book That Made Your World: How the Bible Created the Soul of Western Civilization.* Nashville: Thomas Nelson, 2011.

Rainer, Thom S. *The Unexpected Journey: Conversations with People Who Turned from Other Beliefs to Jesus.* Grand Rapids, MI: Zondervan, 2009.

13

THE MINIMAL FACTS APPROACH

At this point, one may begin to wonder about objections to the reliability of the New Testament. After all, this book has not considered objections to the reliability of the New Testament. So what about these objections? For example, what about the alleged contradictions in the New Testament?

The initial response is that most objections related to contradictions confuse a contradiction with a difference. Differences do not equal contradictions. Moreover, many of these apparent contradictions have already been addressed in other books, such as *The Big Book of Bible Difficulties*.[1]

Another reason I have not dug too deeply into additional objections is that my primary focus has been on providing the positive considerations. I did so by systematically considering numerous reasons scholars have come to view these writings as largely reliable. Thus I have been able to provide a rather substantial cumulative case based upon these positive considerations.

The main reason, however, I have not focused on those details is that my final consideration has to do with the minimal facts approach. The

[1]Norman L. Geisler and Thomas Howe, *The Big Book of Bible Difficulties: Clear and Concise Answers from Genesis to Revelation* (Grand Rapids, MI: Baker, 2008). See also Michael R. Licona, *Why Are There Differences in the Gospels? What We Can Learn from Ancient Biography* (New York: Oxford University Press, 2016). Licona has another upcoming book on the subject: *Jesus, Contradicted: Why the Gospels Tell the Same Story Differently* (Grand Rapids, MI: Zondervan, forthcoming).

minimal facts approach highlights the exceptionally strong reliability of key Gospel events.[2] Gary Habermas developed this approach, and it has become the most widely used approach when presenting the historical data for Jesus' resurrection.[3] Although this approach focuses on Jesus' resurrection, it could be applied to other areas of Jesus' life, early Christianity, or any other historical event. The approach has been applied to everything from the shroud of Turin to American history.[4]

THE CRITERIA OF HABERMAS'S MINIMAL FACTS APPROACH

Part of the reason for the minimal facts approach's success is that it focuses on events that are not only *highly evidenced* but also *widely agreed on* by scholars from diverse theological backgrounds (conservative, liberal, agnostic, atheist, Jewish, etc.).[5] The minimal facts approach only uses two criteria. They can be simply stated:

1. A minimal fact must be well attested, with multiple lines of evidence.
2. The data must be accepted by virtually all scholars, including the more skeptical ones.

Of these two criteria, the first one is by far the *most important*. The minimal facts approach is emphatically not saying that something is true simply because everyone says so. Rather, it "*considers only those*

---

[2]For the best introduction on the subject, see Gary R. Habermas and Michael Licona, *The Case for the Resurrection of Jesus* (Grand Rapids, MI: Kregel, 2004). For more detailed works, see Gary R. Habermas, *The Risen Jesus and Future Hope* (Lanham, MD: Rowman & Littlefield, 2003); Michael R. Licona, *The Resurrection of Jesus: A New Historiographical Approach* (Downers Grove, IL: IVP Academic, 2010). Especially significant here is Habermas's latest work which is over a thousand pages (!): Gary Habermas, *On the Resurrection, Volume 1: Evidences* (Brentwood, TN: B&H Academic, 2024).

[3]Lydia McGrew, *Hidden in Plain View: Undesigned Coincidences in the Gospels and Acts* (Chillicothe, OH: DeWard, 2017), 220-21.

[4]Tristan Casabianca, "The Shroud of Turin: A Historiographical Approach," *Heythrop Journal* 54, no. 3 (May 2013): 414-23; Peter A. Lillback and Jerry Newcombe, *George Washington's Sacred Fire* (Bryn Mawr, PA: Providence Forum, 2006), 30.

[5]One may wonder, if skeptical scholars think the Bible is unreliable, then how do they acknowledge this-or-that fact? The answer is that scholars use the same historical methods used when dealing with other sources that they believe to have various issues, biases, etc. See also chapter six.

data that are so strongly attested historically that they are granted by nearly every scholar who studies the subject, even the rather skeptical ones."[6]

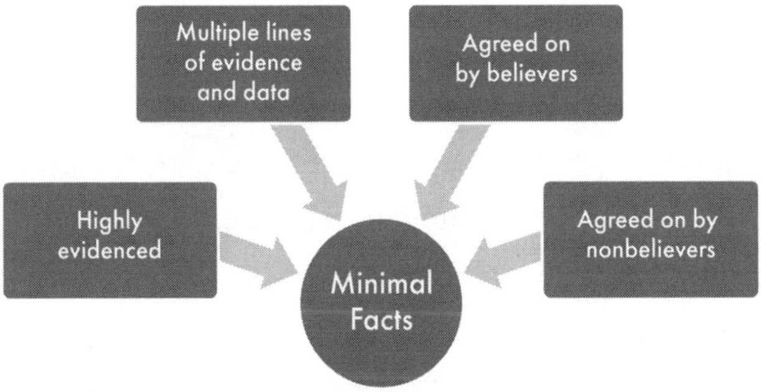

Figure 13.1. The minimal facts approach

The minimal facts approach does not seek to address the reliability question directly. However, there are implicit implications for New Testament reliability since the minimal facts approach uses the historicity of the core events surrounding the message of the gospel. Rather than demonstrating the reliability of the New Testament as a whole, it seeks to highlight the reliability of key Gospel events themselves and work from the bottom up. Accordingly, it avoids most objections that apply to the traditional reliability arguments because it uses data that scholars, including the skeptical ones, *already grant as historical*. In other words, it uses some of the most *reliable* facts.

I should point out that when arguing for the reliability of the New Testament, one is also implying the historicity of the events reported within the New Testament (i.e., the gospel). The minimal facts approach is different because it seeks to establish these events first and is not addressing broader reliability issues. One way to think of the minimal facts approach might be to consider it as the opposite side of the same coin. Both eventually argue for the historicity of the events of the gospel but do so in different ways.

[6]Habermas and Licona, *Case for the Resurrection*, 44, emphasis original.

Introducing some of these highly evidenced and widely agreed-on facts will be helpful. While one's audience will frequently indicate which facts to use, depending on their level of skepticism, some of the most commonly presented facts are the following:[7]

1. Jesus died by crucifixion.
2. The disciples had experiences of the risen Jesus.
3. The disciples were willing to suffer and die for their beliefs.
4. James, Jesus' skeptical brother, converted.
5. Paul, a persecutor of the church, converted.

We also saw in chapter five (Creedal Traditions) that there is wide agreement that this information is reported very early. One can see that there is a connection between these historical data points and those in the creed beginning in 1 Corinthians 15:3 (death, appearances, etc.). Occasionally, the empty tomb is also discussed in this context as well, though with qualification and nuance.[8]

AN EXAMPLE: JESUS' DEATH BY CRUCIFIXION

With these things in mind, let us unpack this argument by focusing on one of these facts to help illustrate how the minimal facts approach works. Consider one of the clearest examples: Jesus' death by crucifixion. I will be able to only briefly present some of the multiple lines of evidence for this minimal fact, but they are:

- ***Multiply attested:*** Jesus' death by crucifixion is reported in an extraordinary number of sources. Not only is it mentioned throughout New Testament sources (Gospels, Paul's writings,

---

[7]For three different lists in two works, see Habermas, *Risen Jesus*, 9-10, 26-27; Habermas and Licona, *Case for the Resurrection*, 43-77. More recently, Habermas, *On the Resurrection*, 1:283-747.

[8]See, for example, the qualifications in Habermas and Licona, *Case for the Resurrection*, 69-74. Although they do not consider it a minimal fact, it is considered a "plus one." The reason it is a "plus one" is because it is less accepted than the others, with around 75 percent acceptance. Nevertheless, this remains quite a large percentage of acceptance among scholars, especially given the debated subject. Moreover, recent figures indicate an even higher percentage of agreement among scholars (Habermas, *On the Resurrection*, 1:632).

etc.), but it is also mentioned in multiple non-Christian sources (e.g., Tacitus, *Annals* 15.44).

- ***Reported early:*** Jesus' death is reported in the earliest Gospel, Mark, as well as in Paul's writings, which are earlier still. Moreover, it is reported in the early creeds and hymns, such as the highly respected formula in 1 Corinthians 15:3, which is typically dated to the early 30s AD.
- ***Embarrassing in nature:*** Paul recognizes the embarrassing nature of crucifixion in 1 Corinthians 1:23. He points out that Jesus' crucifixion was a stumbling block to Jews and foolishness to Gentiles. For Jews, Deuteronomy 21:22-23 says that anyone who is hung on a tree is cursed by God. For Gentiles, crucifixion was the type of death reserved for slaves and lower classes.
- ***"Strauss critique":*** David Strauss was a critic of Christianity who lived in the nineteenth century and is widely considered to have defeated the swoon theory (i.e., that Jesus did not actually die on the cross). In short, his argument states that if Jesus had survived the cross, it would have been *impossible* for him—being bloodied, swollen, bruised, and beaten—to convince the disciples that he conquered the grave and was the Prince of Life.[9]

While several other lines of evidence could be added, the four presented are sufficient for the present purposes.[10] These lines of evidence have convinced virtually all scholars across a wide theological spectrum that Jesus' death is a historical fact. Consistent with the second criterion of the minimal facts approach, scholars who accept Jesus' death include, but are not limited to, the following:

- John Dominic Crossan: "That he was crucified is as sure as anything historical can ever be."[11]

---

[9]David F. Strauss, *A New Life of Jesus*, 2nd ed. (London: Williams and Norgate, 1879), 408-12.

[10]Other examples include the process of crucifixion itself, the spear wound, medical assessments, and other historical criteria (e.g., multiple forms, dissimilarity, etc.).

[11]John Dominic Crossan, *Jesus: A Revolutionary Biography* (San Francisco: HarperSanFrancisco, 1994), 145.

- Craig Keener: "To claim that Jesus died by crucifixion is also not controversial. . . . [Jesus' followers] would not have invented it. Following a leader crucified for treason made the followers themselves liable to the same charge."[12]
- James D. G. Dunn: "That Jesus was crucified on the direct authority of Pilate himself need not be doubted for a minute."[13]
- Bart Ehrman: "The most certain element of the tradition about Jesus is that he was crucified on the orders of the Roman prefect of Judea, Pontius Pilate. The crucifixion is independently attested in a wide array of sources and is not the sort of thing that believers would want to make up."[14]
- Shimon Gibson: "What seems certain is that the crucifixion took place during Pontius Pilate's governorship of Judea, between 26–36 CE, and while Caiaphas was serving as the Jewish High Priest in Jerusalem, between 18–36 CE."[15]
- Pinchas Lapide: "The death of Jesus . . . may be considered historically certain."[16]
- Brant Pitre: "If we know anything about Jesus of Nazareth, it is that he was put to death by crucifixion."[17]

Here we see several authors from vastly different backgrounds theologically, all of whom are persuaded by the multitude of evidence that Jesus died by crucifixion.

The above illustrates how the minimal facts approach works in practice for Jesus' death. When combined with other facts, a strong case

[12]Craig S. Keener, *The Historical Jesus of the Gospels* (Grand Rapids, MI: Eerdmans, 2009), 323.

[13]James D. G. Dunn, *Jesus Remembered: Christianity in the Making* (Grand Rapids, MI: Eerdmans, 2003), 1:775.

[14]Bart D. Ehrman, *The New Testament: A Historical Introduction to the Early Christian Writings*, 3rd ed. (New York: Oxford University Press, 2004), 256.

[15]Shimon Gibson, *The Final Days of Jesus: The Archaeological Evidence* (New York: HarperOne, 2009), 7.

[16]Pinchas Lapide, *The Resurrection of Jesus: A Jewish Perspective* (Eugene, OR: Wipf & Stock, 2002), 32.

[17]Brant Pitre, *The Case for Jesus: The Biblical and Historical Evidence for Christ* (New York: Image, 2016), 156.

for the gospel is built on the reliability of these specific events. There will be minimal objections to these facts, since they receive wide scholarly support. Moreover, the minimal facts have repeatedly raised problems for alternative theories that try to account for the data, with the exception of Jesus' resurrection.[18] This approach has been so effective that Angus Menuge recently wrote that the minimal facts approach explains why "one skeptical alternative after another to the historical fact of the resurrection has been abandoned, leaving critics with shrinking cover to hide from Christ's claim on their life."[19] In other words, these few facts have been incredibly, and surprisingly, difficult for alternative theories to account for while Jesus' resurrection explains them comfortably.

Thus, we have yet another angle supporting the reliability of the events reported in the New Testament.[20] This angle is one that is able to avoid certain rabbit trails and focus on the gospel itself. Concerns regarding alleged contradictions, while important, can be taken into account and reserved for later discussions, while focus given to that which is of "first importance" according to Paul. Once these central events have been addressed, we can then move to other reliability considerations.[21] If we consider the traditional reliability approach to be top down, we might consider the minimal facts approach as building from the bottom up. Again, they are two sides of the same coin.

KEY TAKEAWAYS: MINIMAL FACTS APPROACH

- The minimal facts approach uses two criteria: (1) facts that are supported by multiple lines of historical reasoning and (2) facts that are widely agreed on by scholars from various backgrounds (from skeptics to believers).

[18] Habermas and Licona, *Case for the Resurrection*, 81-150. For a helpful chart, see H. Wayne House and Joseph M. Holden, *Charts of Apologetics and Christian Evidences* (Grand Rapids, MI: Zondervan, 2006), chart 58.

[19] Angus Menuge, "Debating Christian Theism (Book Review)," *Philosophia Christi* 16, no. 2 (2014): 456.

[20] See Habermas, *Risen Jesus*, 89-169.

[21] This was in fact the move of the author, as these arguments were systematically presented after having studied the minimal facts approach first.

- The minimal facts approach uses a bottom-up approach that begins with the most *reliable* events.
- The minimal facts approach is one of the most popular and effective ways of presenting and discussing Jesus' resurrection.

RECOMMENDED READING

Habermas, Gary. *On the Resurrection, Volume 1: Evidences*. Brentwood, TN: B&H Academic, 2024.

Habermas, Gary R., and Michael Licona. *The Case for the Resurrection of Jesus*. Grand Rapids, MI: Kregel, 2004.

Licona, Michael R. *The Resurrection of Jesus: A New Historiographical Approach*. Downers Grove, IL: IVP Academic, 2010.

CONCLUSION AND FINAL THOUGHTS

We have covered a lot of territory throughout this work and done so very quickly. We examined the New Testament from both zoomed-out and zoomed-in perspectives. This enabled us to consider the landscape of the New Testament from these different vantage points. We are also in a better position to understand why James Charlesworth is able to say, as noted above, that there are "too many international authorities to mention" who recognize that "in its broad outline" the Gospels' portrayal of Jesus is "reliable and true."[1]

The cumulative case presented here is rather robust, and we should recall the various arguments covered. By way of summary, we considered:

1. ***New Testament textual evidence:*** We can reasonably believe the words in the New Testament are those that were originally written.
2. ***New Testament genres and audience expectations:*** The Gospels are Greco-Roman biographies and were not expected to freely invent materials (like novels would), while Paul's writings were in-house discussions that were not considered to be forms of propaganda addressed to nonbelievers.

[1]James H. Charlesworth, "Jesus Research Expands with Chaotic Creativity," in *Images of Jesus Today*, ed. James H. Charlesworth and Walter P. Weaver (Valley Forge, PA: Trinity Press International, 1994), 7. Beyond the Gospels, we also observed the value of the writings of one who used to persecute the church—Paul.

3. ***New Testament dating:*** The New Testament documents, particularly the Gospels and Pauline works, were written within the lifetimes of the disciples.
4. ***New Testament authorship:*** The four names associated with the four Gospels are the only four names ever to be associated with them, and even skeptics recognize seven "undisputed" Pauline writings.
5. ***New Testament creedal traditions:*** Creeds, early traditions that concisely summarize the beliefs of the earliest church, are often associated with the apostles and dated to the early 30s AD.
6. ***Historical criteria:*** These criteria evaluate the probability of the historicity of an event, and several key events in the New Testament meet a multitude of these criteria.
7. ***Undesigned coincidences:*** Undesigned coincidences are like puzzle pieces that come together to help illuminate a bigger picture.
8. ***Archaeology:*** Various archaeological findings contribute to the verisimilitude of the New Testament.
9. ***Non-Christian sources:*** These sources have no vested interest in Christianity or its beliefs and yet offer multiple points of confirmation of the New Testament.
10. ***Noncanonical Christian sources:*** These noncanonical sources offer additional insight and corroboration of New Testament texts.
11. ***New Testament canon and credibility:*** The early church recognized the authoritative nature of the New Testament writings, while accepting the best historical sources and rejecting disreputable sources.
12. ***Spiritual and life transformation:*** If the specific teachings of the New Testament are true, then it would be consistent for the lives of individuals throughout history to be changed as a result.
13. ***Minimal facts approach:*** The minimal facts approach uses historical events that are so highly evidenced that they have convinced a large majority of scholars from wide-ranging theological backgrounds, including skeptical ones.

Each of these topics has been covered in detail by various academic journal articles, dissertations, and/or book-length treatments. Accordingly, these chapters were necessarily meant to be a brief introduction to those who are unfamiliar with these aspects of the New Testament along with the different methods used in assessing its claims.

I have introduced a significant case for the reliability of the NT by systematically presenting each of these consideration and presenting a better understanding of what the NT landscape looks like. As Vishal Mangalwadi noted in chapter eleven, not only do we interpret these writings, but these writings interpret us. When we understand that these claims are reliable and that Jesus rose from the dead, this means something not just about Jesus but also about us and for. Having grown in our understanding of the New Testament, we must now consider how we are to move forward in light of these claims. Moreover, these are claims that have withstood continuous and rigorous scholarly critique. As Robert Bowman and Ed Komoszewski point out,

> *There is not a single well-evidenced historical fact about Jesus that undermines the "orthodox" view of Jesus.* Nearly two and a half centuries of assiduous study, research, and discovery by archaeologists, historians, textual critics, and other scholars searching for an alternative Jesus have failed to turn up a scrap of evidence that contravenes what Christians have traditionally said about him. . . . The lack of any well-supported facts that contradict the biblical portrayals of Jesus in the Gospels accepted by the church is no minor manner.[2]

To those considerations, we might also add twelve data points discussed in great detail in Gary Habermas's recent work on Jesus' resurrection.[3] These historical arguments become even more robust when

---

[2]Robert M. Bowman Jr. and J. Ed Komoszewski, "The Historical Jesus and the Biblical Church: Why the Quest Matters," in *Jesus, Skepticism and the Problem of History: Criteria and Context in the Study of Christian Origins*, ed. Darrell L. Bock and J. Ed Komoszewski (Grand Rapids, MI: Zondervan Academic, 2019), 23-24, emphasis original.

[3]Gary Habermas, *On the Resurrection, Volume 1: Evidences* (Brentwood, TN: B&H Academic, 2024).

combined with arguments for God's existence as found in a 2018 publication by Oxford University Press titled *Two Dozen (or So) Arguments for God.*[4]

Since we have looked at reasons why the New Testament is reliable, and are reflecting about what that means for us, it seems fitting to close the discussion with some words from the Gospel of John. In John 20:31, he writes that he has "written so that you may believe that Jesus is the Christ, the Son of God; and that by believing you may have life in His name." We may now read these words, along with the rest of the New Testament, with a new appreciation for their reliability. Indeed, they are trustworthy.

[4]Jerry Walls and Trent Dougherty, *Two Dozen (or So) Arguments for God: The Plantinga Project* (Oxford: Oxford University Press, 2018). Others include Colin Ruloff and Peter Horban, *Contemporary Arguments in Natural Theology: God and Rational Belief* (New York: Bloomsbury, 2021); William Lane Craig and J. P. Moreland, eds., *The Blackwell Companion to Natural Theology* (Malden, MA: Wiley-Blackwell, 2009). For a more introductory work, see William Lane Craig, *On Guard: Defending Your Faith with Reason and Precision* (Colorado Springs: David C. Cook, 2010).

SCRIPTURE INDEX